LOVE

LOVE

by
Miriam Zellnik

RUNNING PRESS
PHILADELPHIA • LONDON

© 2003 by Miriam Zellnik
All rights reserved under the Pan-American and
International Copyright Conventions
Printed in China

*This book may not be reproduced in whole or in part, in any
form or by any means, electronic or mechanical, including
photocopying, recording, or by any information storage and
retrieval system now known or hereafter invented, without
written permission from the publisher.*

9   8   7   6   5   4   3   2
Digit on the right indicates the number of this printing
Library of Congress Control Number 2002095665
ISBN 0-7624-1548-7

Cover design by Bill Jones
Interior design by Jan Greenberg
Edited by Joelle Herr and Nancy Armstrong
Typography: Stone

This book may be ordered by mail from the publisher.
Please include $2.50 for postage and handling.
But try your bookstore first!

Running Press Book Publishers
125 South Twenty-second Street
Philadelphia, Pennsylvania 19103-4399

Visit us on the web!
www.runningpress.com

In Memory of
Julia M. Harrison

(1973–2002)

ACKNOWLEDGMENTS

Special thanks to all the friends and family who allowed me to pester them incessantly for stories about their love lives, as well as for suggestions of favorite romantic scenes in books, movies, and song. I could not have finished this without you! Additional thanks to all the great editors I worked with at Running Press, especially Lynn Rosen, Joelle Herr, and Nancy Armstrong. And thanks always to Adrian, for being so understanding and supportive; I love you!

Contents

INTRODUCTION

Love, sweet love, is a topic of endless fascination, and has been since the earliest recorded literature. Naturally, it is entrancing when we fall in love ourselves, but that doesn't explain why we seek out stories of other people's loves and passions. Perhaps by reading stories of hope and heartbreak, or by learning about love traditions around the world, we seek to make order of our own chaotic and sometimes messy love lives.

Love is many things: a compendium of little-known facts and terminology about romance, an anthology of writings by authors both famous and obscure, a repository of advice from some old-fashioned "self-help" books, and a practical reference that puts useful information—from dating tips to standard wedding vows—at your fingertips.

As I worked on this book, I explored the many sides of love, approaching the subject both as writer and as literary detective, so to speak, mining literature and research materials for the many quotations, facts, and stories contained herein. The book starts with the first steps of finding a date and explores the thrills of a new romance. Moving on, you'll find advice about keeping love alive, including help writing the perfect love letter. You'll take a look at commitment vows from a variety of cultures and learn about wedding facts and traditions throughout history. Midway through the book, you'll find a section on the "sexy stuff," filled with fun facts about the arts of sensual love. And of course, no book of love would be complete without a glance at the darker side of love, including stories about bad dates and breakups, and facts about divorce. Finally, the book ends with a look at a variety of love-related topics such as the history of Valentine's Day, the meanings of flowers, and a why we use hearts to symbolize love.

I hope you'll come to think of this book as a friendly companion, one filled with interesting tales and erudite quotations, and also as a fount of useful information to reference again and again. Whether you're looking for a good quotation to use as a wedding toast or you want to know what movie to rent for an important second date, *Love* will surely become your trusted resource for matters of the heart.

May your days be filled with kisses and your nights with even more.

—Miriam Zellnik

CHAPTER 1

Embarking on Love

[Love is] the name of the sublimest emotion.

—Bernard Talmey, M.D.

There is no sweeter anticipation than the first flowering of love, when two strangers meet and the possibility of true love is in the air. From great literature to present-day anecdotes, it is endlessly fascinating to read about how couples met each other, and this chapter is chock-full of stories about it!

Join Tom Sawyer and Becky Thatcher in their first flush of schoolyard love. Thrill with Levin in Tolstoy's *Anna Karenina* as he realizes the depth of his feelings for his beloved Kitty. In addition to romantic readings, there are suggestions here for first-date plans (as well as a few cautions of things *not* to do on a first date), and even a list of movies especially recommended for the early stages of courtship.

What's that? You're not going out on too many dates lately? Well, if you want to jump-start your social life, check out the ABCs of meeting a mate for a few ideas (twenty-six of them, to be exact). You'll also read what some long-ago authors advised to help people navigate the tricky world of dating—which in some ways has changed very little in the last century. On the other hand, some of their advice sounds downright ridiculous to our modern sensibility.

Back to the present, if you're unsure of how to jump into the fray of online personal ads, the advice here may help you write the ad that lures your true love to your email inbox. This chapter is all about finding love: how other people have done it, and how you can do it too.

Anna Karenina
BY COUNT LEO TOLSTOY

In one moment, as her carriage pulls away, Levin realizes that he loves Kitty after all.

. . . Without wondering who it could be, he gazed absently at the coach. In the coach was an old lady dozing in one corner, and at the window, evidently only just awake, sat a young girl holding in both hands the ribbons of a white cap.

With a face full of light and thought, full of a subtle, complex inner life, that was remote from Levin, she was gazing beyond him at the glow of the sunrise. At the very instant when this apparition was vanishing, the truthful eyes glanced at him. She recognized him, and her face lighted up with wondering delight. He could not be mistaken. There were no other eyes like those in the world. There was only one creature in the world that could concentrate for him all the brightness and meaning of life. It was she. It was Kitty.

He understood that she was driving to Ergushovo from the railway station. And everything that had been stirring Levin during that sleepless night, all the resolutions he had made, all vanished at once. He recalled with horror his dreams of marrying a peasant girl. There only, in the carriage that had crossed over to the other side of the road, and was rapidly disappearing, there only could he find the solution of the riddle of his life, which had weighed so agonizingly upon him of late. 🌼

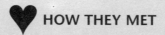

HOW THEY MET

A friend in college met her husband through *The Dating Game,* but she wasn't on the show. She was watching it on TV! She thought Bachelor #2 was cute and seemed cool, although the woman on the show picked Bachelor #1. She lived in NYC and *The Dating Game* was filmed in L.A., so she contacted *The Dating Game* studios and asked for Bachelor #2's phone number.

The *The Dating Game* people, of course, would not give it to her, but when she explained why she wanted it they agreed to pass on her phone number to Bachelor #2. He called her, they arranged to meet, and started a long-distance romance. After some period of time they got married. Have no idea whatever happened to them but I was definitely in awe of her determination to get herself a date!

—Carol Gould

Pickup Lines

Okay, actually most of these are pretty bad, but then again, maybe some would work if given the right ironic spin. However, the publisher of this book bears no responsibility if you try one of these lines and get a slap in response:

- "Your eyes would look great on our kids."

- "Come here often?"

- "What's a nice guy (girl) like you doing in a place like this?"

- "I've slept with 99 girls (guys). Do you want to be 100?"

- "What would you like for breakfast?" (said at dinner)

- "Oh, good, I see you're on the Pill!"

- "Can I find out if you're really a redhead?"

- "Wow, you could be a stripper!"

- "Are those space pants you're wearing? 'Cause your ass is out of this world!"

- "Are those mirrors on your jeans? 'Cause I can see myself in your pants!"

- "Hey, can I bum a cigarette?"

- "Let's get something straight between us."

- "Are your legs tired? 'Cause you've been running through my mind all night."

- "Did it hurt?" ("Did what hurt?") "The bump when you fell down from Heaven."

- "Who's your orthodontist?"

- "What's your zip code?"

ADVICE TO YOUNG WOMEN
SEEKING A MATE

The Royal Path of Life:
Aims and Aids to Success
and Happiness

BY T.L. HAINES, A.M. AND L.W. YAGGY, ©1882

Few things are more amusing to modern eyes than an "advice book" of over a hundred years ago. We roll our eyes and thank our lucky stars we no longer live in such a sexist, restrictive society. The selections below are no exception, and yet, between the lines of the stodgy—and in some cases offensive—advice, there are little gems of wisdom still applicable today.

WHAT ARE A WOMAN'S GREATEST GIFTS?

A woman has no natural gift more bewitching than a sweet laugh. It is like the sound of flutes upon the water. It leads from her in a clear sparkling rill; and the heart that hears it feels as if bathed in the cool, exhilarating spring.

• • •

No trait of character is more valuable in a female than the possession of a sweet temper. Home can never be made happy without it. It is like the flowers that spring up in our pathway, reviving and cheering us. Let a man go home at night, wearied and worn by the toils of the day and how soothing is a word by a good disposition! It is sunshine falling on his heart. He is happy, and the cares of life are forgotten. Nothing can be more touching than to behold a woman who had been all tenderness and dependence, and alive to every trivial roughness while treading the prosperous path of life, suddenly rising in mental force to be the comforter and supporter of her husband under misfortune, and abiding with unshrinking firmness the bitterest winds of adversity.

• • •

A woman of true intelligence is a blessing at home, in her circle of friends, and in society. Wherever she goes, she carries with her a health-giving influence. There is a beautiful harmony about her character that at once inspires a respect which soon warms into love. The influence of such a woman upon society is of the most salutary kind. She strengthens right principles in the virtuous, incites the selfish and indifferent to good actions, and gives to even the light and frivolous a taste for food more substantial than the frothy gossip with which they seek to recreate their minds.

BEAUTY IS BAD

Beauty is a dangerous gift. It is even so. Like wealth it has ruined its thousands. Thousands of the most beautiful women are destitute of common sense and common humanity. No gift from heaven is so general and so widely abused by woman as the gift of beauty. In about nine cases in ten it makes her silly, senseless, thoughtless, giddy, vain, proud, frivolous, self-ish, low, and mean. "She is beautiful, and she knows it," is as much as to say she is spoiled. A beautiful girl is very likely to believe she was made to be looked at; and so she sets herself up for a show at every window, in every door, on every corner of the street, in every company at which opportunity offers for an exhibition of herself. And believing and acting thus, she soon becomes good for nothing else, and when she comes to be a middle-aged woman she is the weakest, most sickening of all human things—a faded beauty.

These facts have long since taught sensible men to beware of beautiful women—to sound them carefully before they give them their confidence. Beauty is shallow—only skin-deep; fleeting—only for a few years' reign; dangerous—tempting to vanity and lightness of mind; deceitful—dazzling often to bewilder; weak—reigning only to ruin; gross—leading often to sensual pleasure. And yet we say it need not be so. Beauty is lovely and ought to be innocently possessed. It is a delightful gift, which ought to be received with gratitude and worn with grace and meekness. It should always minister to inward beauty. Every woman of beautiful form and features should cultivate a beautiful mind and heart.

WHAT IS WRONG WITH YOUNG WOMEN TODAY?

Here our authors get to the crux of the problem: Most young women do not have a strong enough moral backbone to control the men around them.

Young women ought to hold a steady moral sway over their male associates, so strong as to prevent them from becoming such lawless rowdies. Why do they not? Because they do not possess sufficient force of character. They have not sufficient resolution and energy of purpose. Their virtue is not vigorous. Their moral wills are not resolute. Their influence is not armed with executive power. Their goodness is not felt as an earnest force of benevolent purpose. Their moral convictions are not regarded as solemn resolves to be true to God and duty, come what may.

This is the virtue of too many women. They would not have a drunkard for a husband, but they would drink a glass of wine with a fast young man. 🌹

 The Blue Lagoon: A Romance
BY H. DE VERE STACPOOLE

Published in January 1908, *The Blue Lagoon* was an immediate hit with critics and readers alike. One reviewer gushed: "[This] tale of the discovery of love, and innocent mating, is as fresh as the ozone that made them strong." The novel was reprinted more than twenty times in the next twelve years and remained popular in other forms for more than eighty years. Film versions of the novel were made in 1923, 1949, and 1980.

The scene below is a pivotal moment in the story, when castaways Emmeline and Dick discover their true feelings for one another as they take a walk and picnic beside a large statue near their new home.

The "stone man" was the name Emmeline had given the idol of the valley; and sometimes at nights, when her thoughts would stray that way, she would picture him standing all alone in the moonlight or starlight staring straight before him.

He seemed forever listening; unconsciously one fell to listening too, and then the valley seemed steeped in a supernatural silence. He was not good to be alone with.

Emmeline sat down amidst the fears just at his base. When one was close up to him he lost the suggestion of life, and was simply a great stone which cast a shadow in the sun.

Dick threw himself down also to rest. Then he rose up and went off amidst the guava bushes, plucking the fruit and filling his basket. Since he had seen the schooner, the white men on her decks, her great masts and sails, and general appearance of freedom and speed and unknown adventure, he had been more than ordinarily glum and restless. Perhaps he connected her in his mind with the far-away vision of the Northumberland, and the idea of other places and lands, and the yearning for change [that] the idea of them inspired.

He came back with his basket full of the ripe fruit, gave some to the girl and sat down beside her. When she had finished eating them she took the cane that he used for carrying the basket and held it in her hands. She was bending it in the form of a bow when it slipped, flew out and struck her companion a sharp blow on the side of his face.

Almost on the instant he turned and slapped her on the shoulder. She stared at him for a moment in troubled amazement, a sob came in her throat. Then some veil seemed lifted, some wizard's wand stretched out, some mysterious vial broken. As she looked at him like that, he suddenly and fiercely clasped her in his arms. He held her like this for a moment, dazed, stupefied, not knowing what to do with her. Then her lips told him, for they met his in an endless kiss. ❧

HOW THEY MET

My mother was teaching a seminar and my father was a student. He liked her, so he kept asking as many questions as he could think of. After the class had ended, he asked her out on a date, but she thought he must not be very bright—since he had been asking so many simple questions—so she said no. Luckily for me, my father was a persistent fellow, and eventually he convinced her to go out with him!

—Rita Tannenbaum

ADVICE TO YOUNG MEN SEEKING A DATE

In 1937, an excellent tome for men was published, titled *Let's Make Mary: Being A Gentleman's Guide to Scientific Seduction in Eight Easy Lessons*, by Jack Hanley. In this instructional manual, containing such sections as "Selecting a Subject" and "(What to Do) When She Says Yes," the author goes through all the steps involved in seducing a woman, 1930s-style.

In a section titled "Is she conscious of your charms?" Hanley outlines the various methods of acquiring charm, top among them being to "get hold of a million dollars." But in his humorous fashion, he continues, "Very well, then, is she conscious of your charm? Approaching seduction as we are, in a true scientific spirit we must go one step further and inquire: Is she conscious at all?" He suggests asking a girl, to see if she is awake, who the first Stuart ruler of England was.

His scientific methods include a formal list of "systems of seduction" that—according to Hanley—have passed the most rigorous tests of scientific enquiry. Or as he puts it: "So far we have discussed the more general aspects of seduction; now let us be more particular. Or more specific, if you can't afford to be particular."

So without further ado, here are the four systems that he claims are surefire ways for a man to find a willing woman:

1. The Fuddle-Duddle, or Have You a Hollow Leg: This method involves feeding your subject copious amounts of scotch, at which point she becomes so fuddle-duddled that "nature takes over."

2. The Mustache-Twirling, or Ah There, m'Little Beauty (which includes "Come and see my etchings" and other lines): In this method, the seducer plays the "Big Bad Wolf," as it were, since it is a well-known fact that women love bad boys.

3. The Conditional, or I Can Take You Out of All of This: All this method requires is that the seducer be full of empty promises, such as "I can make you a star," or "I can buy you diamonds."

4. The Palsy-Walsy, or Let's Get Together: According to this method, by using an air of camaraderie, the "emancipated" woman is easily won over.

Do not attempt the above methods without adequate training, or disastrous results may occur. An improperly used Fuddle-Duddle, for example, could be the ruin of you.

♥ HOW THEY MET

It was a blind date. My mother had just had her wisdom teeth out, and was over at a friend's house. The friend was going to a dance, and they needed someone to be the date for her boyfriend's friend, so my mother was persuaded to borrow a party dress and go, even though she felt lousy from her oral surgery. The dress was two sizes too big, and she didn't have any shoes that fit so she wore her penny loafers! She refused to dance, and just sat there feeling horrible. The next week, her "date" called her and said he had had a great time (sitting there doing nothing) and that she had the most beautiful brown eyes he ever saw (she has blue eyes). Despite this, she married him.

—Trixie Anderson

JUST PLAIN
DUBIOUS ADVICE

 LOVE, A Treatise on the Science of Sex-Attraction

BY BERNARD S. TALMEY, M.D.

It is not necessarily a bad thing that the name Bernard Talmey, self-appointed moral expert, has been lost to the mists of time. He had the hubris to title his 1919 book *LOVE*, in all capital letters, mind you, and within it he first looks at the ideal qualities of man and woman, as well as describing his horror at the idea of homosexual relationships. The fact that this tome was published by The Eugenics Publishing Company says it all: Eugenics was the pseudo-science that believed you could determine human traits by racial characteristics; unsurprisingly, it was a favorite of the Nazis.

THE INSTINCT OF SEX ATTRACTION

Generally bodily perfection and a retiring, tender, beneficent, confiding nature in woman constitute an attractive ideal for the man, while mental superiority in man constitutes the attracting power for the cultured woman. In her love, the regard for masculine beauty usually forms an unimportant ingredient. The woman, says Kant, has an exquisite feeling for the beautiful, so far as she herself is concerned, but for the noble so far as it is found in man. The man, on the contrary, has a decided feeling for the noble, which belongs to his own qualities, but for the beautiful so far as it is met with in the woman. Hence it follows that the aims of nature are directed through love upon making men still nobler and women more beautiful.

The masculine virtues which impress true women are physical strength, courage, nobility of mind, chivalry, and self-confidence. These virtues constitute the beauty which arouses the woman's love; these are the conspicuous feature of her ideal. The female virtues that impress the man are beauty, tenderness, goodness, refinement, truth, and patience. These are the virtues his ideal possesses.

The more highly cultivated mentally and physically he or she is, the more complex and differentiated are the qualities of their ideals. Hence refined and complex natures experience a great deal of difficulty in meeting with their ideals or any one closely approximating them. But when two happen to complement each other perfectly, when each happens to represent the ideal of the other, then there is true and lasting love. Such people know their ideal when they meet it and have been given time to study it, and they also know that they will never find another one in this world. They know that only this being and no other is suited to them as one triangle is to its congruent.

OBSTACLES TO THE DEVELOPMENT OF LOVE

But true love is possible only if the natural development has not been disturbed or the natural course interrupted, and people have been given the opportunity to develop their ideals. If the development is arrested, if the growth of the erotic instinct is disturbed during puberty, then the mental image of the ideal is confused and the discovery of its organic counterpart is impossible.

Now, the whole nervous system is under great tension during the formation period.

Inquietude, vague unrest and dissatisfaction disturb the boy's equanimity. His heart is tremulous with emotion and represents a volcano of agitation in perpetual eruption. He exudes intense feeling and passion. The mind of the girl is confused with vague dissatisfaction and vaguer desires which she vainly endeavors to define even to herself. Her heart is wildly stirred and issues from its chrysalis to renewed dreams of chimerical bliss. Joy and sorrow, exultation and depression alternate like dawn and dusk. All the complex subtleties of the feminine heart give rein to a single emotion. She lives in the realm of romance, her soul keeps souring in the land of glamour. Hence the least disturbance will be fatal to the development of a clear and distinct image of the ideal.

THE EVILS OF PASSION

True love may really do no evil, but gross passion, which these teachers of the new sex-morality call love, is able to do all the harm in the world. Temporary sexual attraction, which is sensuality pure and simple, is called by the name of love and is made the basis of the new morality. The name of the sublimest emotion which appeals to the noblest sentiments of men and women, which makes chivalrous, gentle, refined and helpful all who are touched by its magic wand, is conferred upon sensuality, as if sensuality ever possessed all these ennobling qualities. ❧

My First Kiss: A Tale of Adolescent Angst

BY MICHAEL HAYNES

Take your mind back to 1979. It's the summer I start junior high and we're in Clarissa Walter's* basement for her thirteenth birthday party. The place is packed and the parents discreetly gone upstairs. There's Ty Mars, all liquid brown eyes and long eyelashes, looking sullen and sleek as he drapes his arm over Lucia Smith's shoulder. At least a half-dozen jealous wallflowers glower unseen at Lucia's good fortune.

There's Philip Mills, his 501 jeans rolled just so and button-up short-sleeved shirt crisp as a two-dollar bill. Philip's as queer as the three-dollar version but none of us knows enough to notice. He's already memorized every one of the parts of *The Wizard of Oz* and his Judy Garland impression is as polished as it will get. None of us realize this until we're juniors, because Philip's black and we don't know black people can be gay.

Over in the corner is Candi Winston, trying her best to cover up her breasts with her folded arms. They are new this year, budding from her cherubic body and drawing the inexorable gaze of nearly every boy in Mr. McKinley's American history class. She looks miserable.

In the middle of the room, standing on a chair is Deirdre Lee. She's trying to get everyone's attention, hands on her hips as she tells everyone to shut up. In three years, she'll be sophomore class president and planning her entry into the sororities of UC-Berkeley. She's on an inside track to leadership class next year and she's already counting her extra curricular activities in a little book that fits so neatly into her Trapper Keeper.

Leaning out the window is Doug Kravits, son of Pete Kravits, owner of King Kovers upholstery. Doug and I are newly minted speed dealers. Doug's older brother Harris learned to un-box diet pills and sell them at a buck apiece to the kids who hang out in the smoking section of Hayward High School. A natural entrepreneur, Harris has Doug and me selling crosstops to our friends: Doug to the future stoners and me to the D&D geeks who desperately want to be mildly dangerous and cool but have no chance in hell. In just four years, I'll be making out with Doug's junior prom date as he lies passed out in the back seat of his brother's SuperSport, a casualty of Bacardi 151 and Deirdre Lee's inexplicable fondness for a scrawny boy who makes her laugh in civics class while Doug is learning to handle sheet metal in voc. ed.

Deirdre Lee finally gets enough people's attention (after Clarissa smacks Manuel Murada and Tom Jamison) and explains that we're going to play Truth or Dare. A slow murmur spreads through the cement-floored basement. Most of us are terrified and excited all at once. Ray Harbin, skinny punk loser with a devilish wit that will turn into a demon's hunger for danger and heroin, rolls his eyes and vanishes out the window with Doug to smoke a joint in the backyard. I look after them and consider following but something keeps me glued to the Naugahyde couch.

It might be the fact that Becky Finn, feather-haired star of my vague and squirmy dreams, is there. Or the chance that someone will dare Candi to show us her bra. I'm not sure what keeps me in that room but I will regret staying there for the next few years of my life.

It starts well enough. Paul Morgan dares Andy Pearsen to lick the floor of the bathroom. Marilyn Tucci makes Deirdre Lee tell us what base she let Rob Hanks get to (second). Harris Cooper has to go into the closet with Linda Meyers and both return flushed. Then Eva Handford spins on Libby Seaton and asks, "Truth or dare?" Libby giggles stupidly and flips her long, straight brown hair back, exposing the feathered roach clip fastened behind her ear. "Dare," she says.

Eva looks around the room and stops on me. I feel a lump rising in my chest. Eva, sensing fear, smiles broadly. "You have to kiss Mike

Haynes!" Libby spins off the couch and faces me. I can remember the zipper of her jeans, curving like a toothy brass grin around the crotch to the back.

"No way! I'm not kissing no ugly guys!"

Now I can tell you that life gets a lot better for me by the time I'm seventeen. I grow from 5'6" to 6'2" and finally shave off that stupid wispy moustache that never quite comes in. I cut off the Ric Ocasek mullet and stop wearing the Def Leppard half-shirts. I get a little more confident and I even get most of the good parts in my high school plays. I learn to drive and to buy beer with my fake ID. And of course, there is the junior prom and Deirdre Lee.

But at that moment, it is all I can do to keep from sinking into the floor. My heart sinks and my face falls with it. I feel my lower lip start to quiver. Somehow I hold it together long enough for someone to throw something at Libby and laugh. "Shut up, Libby!" It's Penelope Pakistanikos and she makes a joke out of it. People laugh and somehow I manage to pretend I don't really care. No one really looks at me and in a few minutes, I can sneak out the front door. It's two more years until my first kiss. Penelope Pakistanikos. 🥀

Names have been changed to protect the mostly innocent. Michael Haynes is a New York-based music industry writer.

HOW THEY MET

My cousin the geologist was at a geologist's convention in Florida and she met this guy. They ended up spending a couple of hours talking to one another, but she had to leave in the morning, and so did he. A day or two later, he called her up and said something to the effect of, "I'm a prospector, I work on my hunches, and my hunch is you are a gold mine. Let's get married." After several months of going out long-distance, they were indeed married.

—Adam G. Gertsacov

 *The Adventures of Tom Sawyer*
BY MARK TWAIN

In this American classic, a young scamp feels the first stirrings of romance in his heart when he meets a girl named Becky Thatcher. In the scene below, Tom has just dazzled her by drawing a picture on his school slate, which she admires.

Tom drew an hour-glass with a full moon and straw limbs to it and armed the spreading fingers with a portentous fan. The girl said:

"It's ever so nice—I wish I could draw."

"It's easy," whispered Tom, "I'll learn you."

"Oh, will you? When?"

"At noon. Do you go home to dinner?"

"I'll stay if you will."

"Good—that's a whack. What's your name?"

"Becky Thatcher. What's yours? Oh, I know. It's Thomas Sawyer."

"That's the name they lick me by. I'm Tom when I'm good. You call me Tom, will you?"

"Yes."

Now Tom began to scrawl something on the slate, hiding the words from the girl. But she was not backward this time. She begged to see. Tom said:

"Oh, it ain't anything."

"Yes it is."

"No it ain't. You don't want to see."

"Yes I do, indeed I do. Please let me."

"You'll tell."

"No I won't—deed and deed and double deed won't."

"You won't tell anybody at all? Ever, as long as you live?"

"No, I won't ever tell *any*body. Now let me."

"Oh, you don't want to see!"

"Now that you treat me so, I *will* see." And she put her small hand upon his and a little scuffle ensued, Tom pretending to resist in earnest but letting his hand slip by degrees till these words were revealed: "I LOVE YOU."

"Oh, you bad thing!" And she hit his hand a smart rap, but reddened and looked pleased, nevertheless.

Just at this juncture the boy felt a slow, fateful grip closing on his ear, and a steady lifting impulse. In that vise he was borne across the house and deposited in his own seat, under a peppering fire of giggles from the whole school. Then the master stood over him during a few awful moments, and finally moved away to his throne without saying a word. But although Tom's ear tingled, his heart was jubilant.

The ABCs of Meeting Mr. or Ms. Right

If you're single, it can be pretty frustrating to have your paired-off friends or family constantly telling you that if you only did this or that thing, you would surely meet the date of your dreams. Inwardly you roll your eyes and think you'll go crazy if you're forced to attend one more "singles" event—or rewrite your personal-ad headline for the fifth time.

Somehow those romantic "meet cute" stories that happen in the movies never seem to happen in your own life. What should you do? Here is a list of places and ideas, designed to spark your own creativity. Some you may have heard before, some ideas may be new to you. And while there's no guarantee that by following these suggestions you'll meet the love of your life, at least you'll get out more!

Answer the phone. This seems simple, but so many of us rely on answering machines and voicemail to screen our calls. Don't be afraid of the phone—pick it up!

Buy yourself a stack of those magazines that you don't usually buy—the expensive glossy ones you save for plane trips—and go sit in a park reading them.

Cast your net wide. Tell everyone you know you'd like to be set up on a blind date.

Dogs are a great way to meet new people, and even if all you meet are a bunch of losers, at least you have a new friend who loves you just for being you. Get a dog.

Eat at restaurants alone. There's nothing wrong

with having a good book as your dinner companion.

Feed the ducks in a local park.

Go back to school. Take a class in something interesting. You might not meet the love of your life, but you might make some new friends who introduce you to more new friends, and so it goes, widening your social circle and upping your chances.

Hairstyle fun: A new cut or color can not only change your appearance but might even shake up your outlook on life. If you've always had long hair, get it chopped. If you favor a short 'do, try a different style or color.

Internships: If you're a college student, what better summer job is there than an internship in your chosen field? It'll further your career and widen your circle.

Join a local conversation salon or book group. Check your local library bulletin board for ideas.

Kites. Go fly one, at a nearby park or beach. Trust me, it will make you smile, and people with kites are approachable.

Love yourself. Sounds trite, but it's true.

Make paper valentines for your friends and co-workers, the more doilies and glitter the better.

Never put yourself down on a date. Self-deprecation only makes people wonder why they're bothering to spend time with you if you keep giving them reasons not to.

Organize a potluck dinner party for friends, and ask everyone to bring at least one new person to introduce to your crowd.

Pick up flowers for yourself, and fill your home with fragrant bouquets.

Quit something—lots of people meet their mates at support groups!

Read a section of the newspaper you usually skip. Breaking out of your routine can have a ripple effect.

Sleep in on the weekend. Sometimes our lives are so busy we don't take the time to relax and catch up on our rest, and a life spent running around all the time is stressful.

Try a new food, something you always assumed you wouldn't like.

Upset the status quo. Wear the wrong attire for a formal party. Bring your dog to a fancy restaurant. Your confidence will be attractive, even if you're asked to leave.

Volunteer for a cause near and dear to your heart. Don't sign up expecting to meet potential dates, but just feel good about doing something you believe in. Your new sense of self-worth will follow you wherever you go.

Wear something from the back of your closet. We all have clothes we love and then forget about. Rediscover old favorites!

Xmarks the spot. Throw a "treasure hunt" party for your friends, with the final destination being a new restaurant or club you've been wanting to try.

Yoga soothes both body and mind. If you've never tried it, find a local class or buy an instructional video.

Zoos are an excellent place to spend a free afternoon. If you're stuck for an interesting idea for a first date, consider this unusual alternative.

HOW THEY MET

A friend of mine from work had been going on the twice-weekly conditioning hikes sponsored by the local Sierra Club chapter. The hikes were intended mainly for "singles" as a way of getting in shape and having an opportunity to meet others in a healthy, low-pressure atmosphere. I hiked with the Sierra Singles for a year, made lots of acquaintances, some friends, and dated several women I met—but no magic had happened. At that point, I learned that Krav Maga, an Israeli martial art, was being taught near where I lived. I enrolled, in spite of the fact the classes conflicted with the hikes (which I had to drop).

After around a year of studying Krav Maga, the instructors announced there would be no class on one particular Thursday. So I decided to make a cameo appearance at the Sierra Club hikes and was literally knocked out when I saw Liz stretching and warming up for the hike. She and I hit it off and got to know each other a bit during the two-hour hike. It turns out that Liz had been going on the hikes for two months before we met, but always on Tuesday. For some odd reason that week, she decided to go on Thursday. Were it not for that quirk of fate, as well as my cancelled Krav Maga class, I would not be writing this story, and I hesitate to imagine what my life would be like.

—Sandy H.

The Royal Path of Life: Aims and Aids to Success and Happiness

BY T.L. HAINES, A.M. AND L.W. YAGGY, ©1882

The ostensible object of courtship is the choice of a companion. *For no other object* should any intercourse having the appearance of courtship be permitted or indulged in. It is a species of high-handed *fraud* upon an unsuspecting heart, worthy of the heaviest penalty of public opinion, or law. He who does it is a *wretch*. He should be ranked among thieves, robbers, villains, and murderers. He who steals money steals trash; but he who steals affections without a return of similar affections steals that which is dearer than life and more precious than wealth. His theft is a robbery of the heart.

Flirting is a *horrid outrage* upon the most holy and exalted feelings of the human soul, and the most sacred and important relation of life. It is a vulgarism and wickedness to be compared only to blasphemy. It had, and still has, its origin in the *basest lust*. The refined soul is always *disgusted* with it. It is awfully demoralizing in its tendency, and low and base in its character.

There is much *trifling courting* among the young in some portions of the county that results in such *calamitous* consequences; carried on sometimes when the young man means nothing but present pleasure, and sometimes when the young woman has not other object in view. Such intercourse is confined mostly to young men *and women before they are of age. It is a crying evil, worthy* of the most severest censure. 🐚

HOW THEY MET

On Easter morning, 1969, shortly after I turned thirty, I went to a gathering in a Manhattan apartment to meet some people who had offered shares in a weekend summer house on Fire Island, in a *Village Voice* ad. I chatted to various people, in particular, a pretty 28-year-old English woman I had noticed as I entered. I still remember my first sight of her, sitting with her back against a wall, dressed in a yellow and blue long-sleeved shirt and blue pants. I asked her for a date. She had a busy social schedule, so it was some time before she would go out with me.

Our first date was a bit rocky; perhaps, as she now puts it, I was a bit arrogant. But after a long walk and my introducing her to *Casablanca*, we began seeing each other, first once a week, then more often, then every night. On June 23, the night of our tenth date, without doing a great deal of thinking about the matter, I suddenly blurted out, "Jessica, can you think of any good reason why we shouldn't get married?"

She coolly replied, "Would you like to rephrase that question?"

I did rephrase the question, and the answer was yes, and since then we have lived happily ever after.

—Henry Townsend

🐦 *My Flirtations*

This Victorian book, first published in 1893, is an eye-opening look at how romance and crushes on handsome strangers hasn't changed a bit in over one hundred years. The book was published under the name Margaret Wynman, a pseudonym for Ella Hepworth Dixon. What follows are a few selected excerpts that detail the lot of interesting young gentlemen who liked to flirt with our poor besotted narrator.

The first one—the very first one? Well, I think it was a sallow, under-sized Italian with handsome ox-eyes, who used to give us violin lessons; or else it was a cousin, a boy with sandy hair, who stammered, and who was reading for the army; but, no, I rather think it was the anxious young doctor, who came when I had the measles—anyhow, he, the primeval one, is lost in the mists of antiquity. . . .

• • •

Tony was a lieutenant in a line regiment, and I fear his high spirits made him have occasional differences of opinion with his colonel. In appearance he was distinctly good to look at. He had a clean, pink skin, twinkling blue eyes, and hair so flaxen that it was almost silver. His shoulders were broad and square, he had a delightful laugh, and he was just three-and-twenty. And, without being in the least conceited, Tony was thoroughly pleased with himself, his regiment, and his belongings. He had, in a supreme degree, the magnetism which comes of perfect health, good spirits, and complete self-satisfaction.

What an infectious thing is happiness, and what a golden age is three-and-twenty! With what vigour did Tony play lawn-tennis, how excited he got over races and cricket matches, how hot he became when he danced, what portentous suppers he could eat! . . . The very sound of his voice in the hall—a voice with raised inflections, for the ends of Tony's sentences always finished joyously—roused one up on the foggiest and dreariest of days.

To go for a walk in the park or along Piccadilly with Tony Lambert was a whole education in itself in the ways of young men: his joy was so manifest when a pretty face, a showy figure, or even a well-cut gown appeared in sight. He had the omnivorous glance which takes in every detail, and which is the prerogative of men who spend most of their leisure in sport. Seldom will you find a writer, a lawyer, or a scientist with the faculty of observation as highly cultivated as in the most brainless individual used to the rod and the gun.

• • •

The gleam of velvety grass through a grey cloister, a bare oaken staircase, leading to a low room lined with books; a cushioned window seat, a summer night, and the distant sound of someone playing the violin: these are the things that come back to me whenever anyone pronounces the name of Frank Harding.

It was at Oxford, at Commemoration, that I saw him first. He was lying on his back on the grass in one of those small, meagre gardens in the Parks which make the joy of Oxford dons and their wives, and their troops of babies. As a matter of fact, he was being photographed—we were all being photographed—as is the pleasing custom during Commemoration week.

Frank Harding was one of those exceptional beings, an undergraduate on easy—nay, even familiar—terms with dons. The wives of these gentlemen were very tolerant of Frank—indeed, if it were given to a don's wife to be capable of a flirtation, I am pretty sure they would have flirted with him. As it was, he strolled in and out of those villas in Norham Gardens very much as he liked, played with the babies, teased the dogs, and helped the ladies of the house in their perennial little difficulties with the Greek syntax. In spite of his eccentricities and those daring caricatures of the dons of his which regularly appeared in Shrimpton's window, the authorities all liked Frank, and everybody was ready to bet—if one can picture such a transaction taking place in a college common-room—that Frank would take a First.

• • •

One of the most amusing things about Mr. Valentine Redmond was his imperturbable coolness. Though hardly two-and-twenty, he had none of the tremors, the diffidences of youth. I have seen him talk to an archbishop or a foreign potentate with the same ease with which he would tackle an undergraduate or take a young lady down to supper. Not that you would ever have caught Val Redmond wasting his acidulous sweetness on a young girl. Women under thirty seldom went to his house.

One of his least pleasing characteristics was a tendency to flout and pout. He was constantly having little quarrels with his intimate friends. His intimate friendships lasted, on an average, exactly six weeks. In other houses where they talk scandal it is usually about acquaintances, but in Val's drawing-room you generally heard his bosom friends deprived of their reputations. This is a trait which makes society feel uneasy, and to it one may perhaps attribute the brief duration of Val's friendships. Ours, for instance, though it was never perfervid, lasted but a brief two months. ✒

HOW THEY MET

My friend Sandy was on jury duty. At the end of the trial they all had a chance to say something to the rest of the jury before they dispersed. She said, "I'm single. If anyone knows anyone. . . ." One of her co-jurors set her up with a friend—and seven months later they got married!

—Tina DeMartin

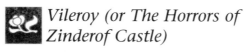

Vileroy (or The Horrors of Zinderof Castle)

BY ELIZABETH CAROLINE GREY

Originally published in 1844, this "penny dreadful" tale of murder and mayhem follows the story of Constance, the beautiful young heroine. In this scene, she is much admired by the soldier, Frederique.

"Father," said Constance, "you know I am happy but for your sake, my heart, indeed, rejoices that hope has again arisen."

"And have you no word of welcome for your father's friend, Constance?" said the chevalier, smiling.

Constance held out her hand timidly to Frederique.

He pressed it respectfully to his lips. What a moment of pure unalloyed happiness was that to the young soldier.

"We will follow you, Constance," said her father to her.

With cheeks glowing with innocent pleasure, the fair Constance tripped before her father and Frederique, the latter of whom followed her every movement with admiring eyes.

"Oh, most rare and exquisite beauty," he mentally soliloquized. "Can it be possible that in the shrinking timidity of thy loveliness, I see likewise her whose bold and resolute spirit yesterday prompted her to snatch a weapon to repel the intruder upon her father's place of refuge? Henceforth, dear Constance, I dedicate my life to thee. Thy name shall be the watchword of my fancy; the thought of thee shall nerve my arm in the battlefield. For thy sake I will earn laurels, and a name among the bravest. Heaven is kind to me, to guide me alone to the shrine of so much grace, so much wondrous beauty; a beauty which might witch the world with wonder; a loveliness on which mankind might gaze for ever unsatiated. Oh, Constance! Constance! Love me, or kill me, there is no medium."

"Why do you sigh, Frederique?" said the Chevalier D'Anville.

"Did I sigh, my friend?" said Frederique, rather confused.

"You did, in faith, and deeply too."

"May I tell you, chevalier, and be forgiven?" said Frederique.

The Chevalier D'Anville did not answer for a moment, and then slacking his pace, he said:

"Yes, Frederique, you may. I do esteem you noble."

"It was a foolish thought," said Frederique,

"but I sighed to think, chivalier [sic], that two days had passed since I have hunted in the forest, and I had missed seeing Constance till the third."

"Frederique," said the chevalier, "I will not affect to misunderstand you. With all the impetuosity of youth, you fancy that you love my daughter." ❧

♥ HOW THEY MET

I was out to dinner with my sister at Marion's in the Bowery in NYC. Sitting next to us was a table of three guys, all cute. It got toward the end of the meal, and I ordered a butterscotch sundae. When it arrived, I asked if they had mixed up my order, because it looked more like hot fudge. They assured me it was just really dark butterscotch. Suddenly, a voice from the next table piped up: "I'll taste it for you."

I said okay, but he said he didn't have a spoon. My sister handed him hers. Then we all started talking, ordering drinks, etc. We all went out after that for more drinks, and my sundae-taster and I sort of fell into step and we even ended up kissing at the bar. We went out the next night and I basically never went home. We ended up dating seriously for several months.

—Jessica Mann Gutteridge

Real-Life Pickup Tales

I always get that tired old, "Haven't I seen you somewhere before?" to which my favorite reply is, "I was an extra in *Porky's*. . . . You may have seen me in the shower scene."

A librarian tells of the best line she ever got: "You must be a library book, 'cause you've got FINE written all over you."

Another library standard (who knew libraries were such hotbeds of cruising?): "I'm glad I have my library card, because I'm checkin' you out!"

One woman describes a pickup line that most definitely did not work: "Some guy once said I looked like his sister."

"A friend and I semi-crashed this party (friend-of-a-friend type of thing). A guy approached us and asks her name. 'Meredith,' she said. He continued, 'So, would that be Ms., Mrs., Miss, or what?' 'Professor,' she replied. The look on his face was priceless; I guess sexism still exists! For what it's worth, he slunk away right after that."

HOW THEY MET

I met Jon in a newsroom—the Atlantic City *Press*, 1969, where he was the ace investigative reporter and I was the summer intern. If only Tracy and Hepburn were still making movies. . . .

—Paula Span

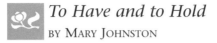

To Have and to Hold

BY MARY JOHNSTON

This 1900 bestselling novel is a historical romance set against the backdrop of early American settlements in 1622. Here, the dashing hero, Captain Ralph Percy, is parted from his wife, the lady Jocelyn, a girl of noble birth who ran away from England and an arranged marriage. Although she gave her hand in marriage to Percy, their love for each other was never fully expressed, and in this scene he has been jailed and she has one last visit with him.

There was a noise outside the door, and Rolfe's voice speaking to the gaoler. Impatient for his entrance I started toward the door, but when it opened he made no move to cross the threshold. "I am not coming in," he said, with a face that he strove to keep grave. "I only came to bring some one else." With that he stepped back, and a second figure, coming forward out of the dimness behind him, crossed the threshold. It was a woman, cloaked and hooded. The door was drawn to behind her, and we were alone together.

Besides the cloak and hood she wore a riding mask. "Do you know who it is?" she asked, when she had stood, so shrouded, for a long minute, during which I had found no words with which to welcome her.

"Yea," I answered: "the princess in the fairy tale."

She freed her dark hair from its covering, and unclasping her cloak let it drop to the floor. "Shall I unmask?" she asked, with a sigh. "Faith! I should keep the bit of silk between your eyes, sir, and my blushes. Am I ever to be the forward one? Do you not think me too bold a lady?" As she spoke, her white hands were busy about the fastening of her mask. "The knot is too hard," she murmured, with a little tremulous laugh and a catch of her breath.

I untied the ribbons.

"May I not sit down?" she said plaintively, but with soft merriment in her eyes. "I am not quite strong yet. My heart—you do not know what pain I have in my heart sometimes. It makes me weep of nights and when none are by, indeed it does!"

There was a settle beneath the window. I led her to it, and she sat down.

"You must know that I am walking in the Governor's garden that hath only a lane between it and the gaol." Her eyes were downcast, her cheeks pure rose.

"When did you first love me?" I demanded.

"Lady Wyatt must have guessed why Master Rolfe alone went not to the bear-baiting, but joined us in the garden. She said the air was keen, and fetched me her mask, and then herself went indoors to embroider Samson in the arms of Delilah."

"Was it here at Jamestown, or was it when we were first wrecked, or on the island with the pink hill when you wrote my name in the sand, or—"

"*The George* will sail in three days, and we are to be taken back to England after all. It does not scare me now."

"In all my life I have kissed you only once," I said.

The rose deepened, and in her eyes there was laughter, with tears behind. "You are a gentleman of determination," she said. "If you are bent upon having your way, I do not know that

I—that I—can help myself. I do not even know that I want to help myself."

Outside the wind blew and the sun shone, and the laughter from below the fort was too far away and elfin to jar upon us. The world forgot us, and we were well content. There seemed not much to say: I suppose we were too happy for words. I knelt beside her, and she laid her hands in mine, and now and then we spoke. In her short and lonely life, and in my longer stern and crowded one, there had been little tenderness, little happiness. In her past, to those about her, she had seemed bright and gay; I had been a comrade whom men liked because I could jest as well as fight. Now we were happy, but we were not gay. Each felt for the other a great compassion; each knew that though we smiled to-day, the groan and the tear might be to-morrow's due; the sunshine around us was pure gold, but that the clouds were mounting we knew full well.

"I must soon be gone," she said at last. "It is a stolen meeting. I do not know when we shall meet again."

She rose from the settle, and I rose with her, and we stood together beside the barred window. There was no danger of her being seen; street and square were left to the wind and the sunshine. My arm was around her, and she leaned her head against my breast. "Perhaps we shall never meet again," she said.

"The winter is over," I answered. "Soon the trees will be green and the flowers in bloom. I will not believe that our spring can have no summer."

She took from her bosom a little flower that

had been pinned there. It lay, a purple star, in the hollow of her hand. "It grew in the sun. It is the first flower of spring." She put it to her lips, then laid it upon the window ledge beside my hand. "I have brought you evil gifts,—foes and strife and peril. Will you take this little purple flower—and all my heart beside?"

I bent and kissed first the tiny blossom, and then the lips that had proffered it. "I am very rich," I said.

The sun was now low, and the pines in the square and the upright of the pillory cast long shadows. The wind had fallen and the sounds had died away. It seemed very still. Nothing moved but the creeping shadows until a flight of small white-breasted birds went past the window. "The snow is gone," I said. "The snow-birds are flying north."

"The woods will soon be green," she murmured wistfully. "Ah, if we could ride through them once more, back to Weyanoke—"

"To home," I said.

"Home," she echoed softly.

There was a low knocking at the door behind us. "It is Master Rolfe's signal," she said. "I must not stay. Tell me that you love me, and let me go."

I drew her closer to me and pressed my lips upon her bowed head. "Do you not know that I love you?" I asked.

"Yea," she answered. "I have been taught it. Tell me that you believe that God will be good to us. Tell me that we shall be happy yet; for oh, I have a boding heart this day!"

Her voice broke, and she lay trembling in my arms, her face hidden. "If the summer never comes for us," she whispered. "Good-by, my lover and my husband. If I have brought you ruin and death, I have brought you, too, a love that is very great. Forgive me and kiss me, and let me go."

"Thou art my dearly loved and honored wife," I said. "My heart forebodes summer, and joy, and peace, and home."

We kissed each other solemnly, as those who part for a journey and a warfare. I spoke no word to Rolfe when the door was opened and she had passed out with her cloak drawn about her face, but we clasped hands, and each knew the other for his friend indeed. They were gone, the gaoler closing and locking the door behind them. As for me, I went back to the settle beneath the window, and, falling on my knees beside it, buried my face in my arms. ❧

HOW THEY MET

My husband David and I met a few times when we were with other people but finally, when we were both single, we met at a volleyball game. He pushed me down backwards over a mutual friend who was kneeling behind me just for that purpose. His schoolyard high jinks must have touched the right chord with me, because we soon went out on our first date, which was this: He asked me for a juggling lesson.

—Brady Lea, professional clown

Lady Audley's Secret, Vol. 1
BY MARY ELIZABETH BRADDON

This 1862 melodrama follows the trials and tribulations of Miss Audley, a woman of mysterious means in search of a husband. While she is enamored of her cousin Robert, in this scene the author explains why all her feminine wiles (including feigning an interest in Robert's friend, the handsome widower George Talboys) will not be helpful to her cause.

So the dinner at Audley Court was postponed, and Miss Alicia had to wait still longer for an introduction to the handsome young widower, Mr. George Talboys.

I am afraid, if the real truth is to be told, there was, perhaps, something of affectation in the anxiety this young lady expressed to make George's acquaintance; but if poor Alicia for a moment calculated upon arousing any latent spark of jealousy lurking in her cousin's breast by this exhibition of interest, she was not so well acquainted with Robert Audley's disposition as she might have been. Indolent, handsome, and indifferent, the young barrister took life as altogether too absurd a mistake for any one event in its foolish course to be for a moment considered seriously by a sensible man.

His pretty, gipsy-faced cousin might have been over head and ears in love with him, and she might have told him so, in some charming, roundabout, womanly fashion, a hundred times a day for all the three hundred and sixty-five days in the year; but unless she had waited for some privileged 29th of February, and walked straight up to him, saying, "Robert, please will you marry me?" I very much doubt if he would ever have discovered the state of her feelings.

Again, had he been in love with her himself, I fancy that the tender passion would, with him, have been so vague and feeble a sentiment that he might have gone down to his grave with a dim sense of some uneasy sensation which might be love or indigestion, and with, beyond this, no knowledge whatever of his state.

So it was not the least use, my poor Alicia, to ride about the lanes round Audley during those three days which the two young men spent in Essex; it was wasted trouble to wear that pretty cavalier hat and plume, and to be always, by the most singular of chances, meeting Robert and his friend. The black curls (nothing like Lady Audley's feathery ringlets, but heavy clustering locks, that clung about your slender brown throat), the red and pouting lips, the nose inclined to be retroussé; the dark complexion, with its bright crimson flush, always ready to glance up like a signal light in a dusky sky, when you came suddenly upon your apathetic cousin—all this coquettish, espiègle, brunette beauty was thrown away upon the dull eyes of Robert Audley, and you might as well have taken your rest in the cool drawing-room at the Court, instead of working your pretty mare to death under the hot September sun.

They met Alicia Audley on her mare about half an hour after they had come to the determination of leaving Essex early the next morning. The young lady was very much surprised and disappointed at hearing her cousin's determination, and for that very reason pretended to take the matter with supreme indifference.

"You are very soon tired of Audley, Robert," she said carelessly; "but of course you have no friends here, except your relations at the Court; while in London, no doubt, you have the most delightful society, and—"

"I get good tobacco," murmured Robert, interrupting his cousin. "Audley is the dearest old place, but when a man has to smoke dried cabbage leaves, you know, Alicia—"

"Then you really are going to-morrow morning?"

"Positively—by the express train that leaves at 10:50."

• • •

"Never mind," said the young lady . . . "Let me go; it's past eight, and I must answer a letter by to-night's post. Come, Atalanta! Good-by, Robert—good-by, Mr. Talboys. A pleasant journey to town."

The chestnut mare cantered briskly through the lane, and Miss Audley was out of sight before those two big bright tears that stood in her eyes for one moment, before her pride sent them back again, rose from her angry heart.

"To have only one cousin in the world," she cried passionately, "my nearest relation after papa, and for him to care about as much for me as he would for a dog!" 🐚

HOW THEY MET

We had met a few times at parties, and even had a class together, but my SO and I actually got together on our first date thanks to a computer program that was an annual tradition at our colleges (Haverford and Bryn Mawr). The program was called Senior Fling, and it worked like this: Every senior's student ID number was placed into a database. Each of them then specified any other students whom they had an interest in "having a fling" with.

The idea was that as seniors prepared to graduate and go out into the world, this was one last chance to hook up with someone they'd had their eye on through all those years of study. All their desired flings were matched up against every other student who had taken the time to enter his or her own choices, and when there was a match, the senior had the option of following up on it.

At any rate, that's how my now-girlfriend and I got together—this is now ten years ago! She sent me a wry email telling me: "We seem to have been matched up by the Senior Fling" program, and the rest is history.

—Barron Pickett

ONLINE DATING SITES

There are so many websites devoted to meeting that special someone. Which one should you use? There's no easy answer to that question, but the best plan is to spend a few hours browsing around sites that interest you, and see if some of the people there seem compatible with you. Often, you'll have to register for a site, but be wary of sites that do not let you browse until you pay. Most reputable sites allow you to look around, and only charge if you want to answer ads or place your own. Also, many sites have free trial memberships; taking advantage of them can help you make a decision before shelling out some cash.

By no means a comprehensive listing, here are a few popular online personals sites:

www.personals.yahoo.com: Your basic personal ads site, available in all regions of the United States and Canada.

www.match.com: Originally catered to a more computer-literate crowd, but now is just a basic site for all kinds of singles.

www.matchmaker.com: Again, a standard site for all sorts of singles.

www.nerve.com: This is a personals site attached to *Nerve* magazine, self-described as "literate smut." Folks here are generally a little more urban and edgy than on more mainstream sites.

WRITING AN EFFECTIVE PERSONAL AD

At the dawn of the Online Dating Age, say all the way back in 1996, the person placing an ad could traditionally pick and choose from amongst a sea of potential admirers. Alas, as more and more websites proliferated, more people went out on bad dates with prospective matches, many of whom—it turned out—had misrepresented themselves.

The age of innocence has ended, and placing an ad is no guarantee that anyone will bother to answer it. The bar is a little higher now. You can't just write any old ad; you have to craft a really *good* ad.

So here are some tricks, tips, and strategies for composing an ad that is eye-catching and honest, an ad that will do the most important things: connect you with the right people and filter out the wrong ones.

1. *Tell the truth.*

Saying you are tall and then showing up on the first date wearing six-inch elevator lifts, or saying you're young when in fact you have an AARP card, is probably not a great strategy for finding true love. If you have something you're uncomfortable about it, don't sugarcoat it, but rather, treat it bluntly and with a sense of humor.

Bad	I need to lose some weight.
Better	I'm an excellent cook, so I'm not what you might call "slender."

2. Be specific.

Mentioning actual books, movies, and music you like is always better than giving broad categories. And describing a perfect date as "a walk on the beach" is far too overused to be interesting. It's true what your seventh-grade English teacher told you: Show, don't tell!

Bad	I like jazz and reading.
Better	Sunday mornings, you'll find me curled up with a good book, Louis Armstrong or Count Basie on the stereo.

3. Describe whom you're looking for.

While it's a good idea to be specific about who you are and what your interests are, it's generally not a good idea to have too narrow a definition of whom you're looking for, since you might inadvertently discourage a worthwhile person from answering.

Bad	Seeking slim brunette who likes Italian food and Ultimate Frisbee.
Better	Seeking athletic woman, the kind of person who's happy to toss around a Frisbee or go for long walks on the weekends.

---

4. Be positive and self-aware.

A quick perusal of any personal ads site reveals a lot of people with very visible baggage, and nothing turns off a prospective date faster than seeing a person's neuroses before you've even met him or her! Much as you might like to "get back at" your last partner by posting a litany of things you *don't* want, resist the temptation.

Bad	No game-players, no stuck-up snobs, no workaholics!
Better	I'm a warm and honest person, looking for the same.

AN INSIDE LOOK AT
POWER DATING

It was bound to come to this. People are busy, and they want results fast—whether it's a microwaved dinner that's ready in 30 seconds or a quick way to size up a pool of potential long-term mates.

It's the new trend that's sweeping the nation! Sometimes called "five-minute dating" or "speed dating," the basic idea is that a roomful of people are paired off with each other, one-on-one. A buzzer sounds at a pre-arranged time interval (usually five to ten minutes), and the couples reshuffle so that each person is talking to someone new.

Many of the companies that organize these events are regional. In addition, different dating events cater to different groups of singles. For example, a New York-based service called Date Bait (www.datebait.com) has three sets of events for straight, gay (male), or lesbian attendees. Within each of these groups, they then have several different specialty events advertised for age ranges (twenties/thirties only, thirties/forties only, etc.) and types of people (professionals only, creative people only, Jewish, etc.).

To find out if speed dating is offered in your area, check your local free weekly for ads about events, or search online at a regional website.

ONE MAN'S STORY: SPEED DATING

Michael Mancilla is a relationship therapist who lives and works in the Washington D.C. area. He is the co-author of the book *Love in the Time of HIV: Gay Men's*

Guide to Sex, Dating, and Relationships, published by Guilford Press in 2003.

He twice participated in Rainbow Dating, a (now defunct) gay matchmaking service that organized speed-dating events. He had this to say about his experiences:

Q: So how was the whole thing organized?

A: Well, both times it was held at this tea shop/coffee shop type place. You have a group of men. There were about six or seven men the times I went, and you all are given name tags and a paper to fill out as you go along. It's a list of all the names of the men there, and different levels of interest you have in them.

Q: So you talk for a certain amount of time?

A: Exactly. The moderator—the "yenta," so to speak—calls your name and names someone else you are matched with, and you sit together talking for seven minutes. Then a bell rings, and you return to your original seats. The moderator calls out different pairings, and you repeat the process, rotating through until you have met all the other people.

Q: So did you have planned questions to ask people? How much preparation did you do before going to this?

A: Well, I took care with what I wore, made sure my shirt was pressed, that kind of thing. And they give you guidelines and suggested topics for conversation: the last movie you saw, what your favorite vacation was. And of course, we all have a repertoire of stories to tell.

Q: So what was it like, rushing around meeting all these new people in this organized way?

A: Well, in some ways it literally brings you

back to seventh grade, the whole "I like you, do you like me?" feeling of it.

Q: So after this, then they match you up, right?

A: You have to mark down whom you would want to go out on another date with. Then they compare your list with the others to see what people you chose had chosen you, and if there's a match, you exchange contact information. The first time I did it, I met seven men, and out of those there were four that I was interested in, and out of those four, two of them wanted to meet with me, so I got two matches.

Q: So would you recommend this to people as a way to meet?

A: Sure! It's a hoot! I mean, there is that element

of "do you like me," as I said before, but it's a good way to cut through the politeness of people giving you a phone number when they really aren't interested, but they don't want to hurt your feelings or whatever. This way, you know both people at least are interested enough to want to get to know each other better.

BEST MOVIES
FOR AN EARLY DATE

There are many wonderful films that are perfect for the beginning stage of courtship, from classics to recent teen faves. Your taste will help determine whether you want something scary (*Scream, Blair Witch Project*) or something sweet

(*Chocolat, Notting Hill*). Here are a few that guarantee to set a romantic mood conducive to cuddling on the couch with a new sweetie:

Say Anything . . . (1989) This paean to first love awakens the romantic in everyone, and the scene where John Cusack holds up a boom box blasting a Peter Gabriel song to try to win back the woman he loves is priceless.

Casablanca (1942) There's a reason this beloved film has endured as a perennial favorite. It's romantic without being sappy, thrilling without being violent, and has beautiful black-and-white cinematography and an amazing cast.

The Quiet Man (1952) In one of his few non-Westerns, John Wayne shines as the romantic American in this sweet film about an Irish courtship.

Other movies that make great date choices for a budding courtship:

Flirting (1991)

Monsoon Wedding (2001)

Amélie (2001)

Chocolat (2000)

The Red Violin (1998)

To Have and Have Not (1944)

Desperado (1995)

Strictly Ballroom (1992)

WORST MOVIES
FOR AN EARLY DATE

After exhaustive research in bad dates, the following three movies win the award for worst movies to watch if you want to get cozy with a new guy or gal:

Happiness (1998) Pedophilia and graphic masturbation scenes don't exactly make for light, flirtatious post-film banter. This Todd Solondz film will have you wincing in no time at all.

Triumph of the Will (1934) It's worth seeing this classic Leni Riefenstahl Nazi propaganda film that spawned the fascist aesthetic; however, it's probably best saved for a later date.

The Lifestyle (1999) Cuddling on the couch will be the last thing you feel like doing after watching this documentary about middle-American swingers in all their sagging glory.

Other films not to reach for at the video store if you want to get another date:

The Cook, the Thief, his Wife and her Lover (1989)

War of the Roses (1989)

Boys Don't Cry (1999)

Breaking the Waves (1996)

Jude (1996)

Straw Dogs (1971)

Blue Velvet (1986)

Sweetie (1989)

♥ HOW THEY MET

I met my SO in the second row of a Grateful Dead show in 1988; we sat next to each other and we still have our stubs. But we were just complete strangers who happened to be sitting next to each other. He resurfaced two years later in the form of a *Village Voice* personal ad. We have been together as a couple ever since.

It's funny, we didn't immediately realize the odd coincidence of our earlier "meeting," but it was soon after we re-met through the *Voice* personal that we were talking about shows we were at, and I was like, "I saw Whoopi Goldberg on stage at the Cap Center [in Landover, MD] and I talked to her from my seat in the second row," and he was like, "I was in the second row and there was this guy talking to Whoopi," and that was me. We pulled out our stubs and it turned out we had had adjacent seats.

—Parker Lawrence

 *Camille*
BY ALEXANDER DUMAS

This famous novel tells the story of a doomed courtesan and her idealistic young lover.

Little by little I had drawn nearer to Marguerite. I had put my arms about her waist, and I felt her supple body weigh lightly on my clasped hands.

"If you knew how much I love you!" I said in a low voice.

"Really true?"

"I swear it."

"Well, if you will promise to do everything I tell you, without a word, without an opinion, without a question, perhaps I will say yes."

"I will do everything that you wish!"

"But I forewarn you I must be free to do as I please, without giving you the slightest details what I do. I have long wished for a young lover, who should be young and not self-willed, loving without distrust, loved without claiming the right to it. I have never found one. Men, instead of being satisfied in obtaining for a long time what they scarcely hoped to obtain once, exact from their mistresses a full account of the present, the past, and even the future. As they get accustomed to her, they want to rule her, and the more one gives them the more exacting they become. If I decide now on taking a new lover, he must have three very rare qualities: he must be confiding, submissive, and discreet."

"Well, I will be all that you wish."

"We shall see."

"When shall we see?"

"Later on."

"Why?"

"Because," said Marguerite, releasing herself from my arms, and, taking from a great bunch of red camellias a single camellia, she placed it in my buttonhole, "because one can not always carry out agreements the day they are signed."

"And when shall I see you again?" I said, clasping her in my arms.

"When this camellia changes colour."

"When will it change colour?"

"To-morrow night between eleven and twelve. Are you satisfied?"

"Need you ask me?"

"Not a word of this either to your friend or to Prudence, or to anybody whatever."

"I promise."

"Now, kiss me, and we will go back to the dining-room."

She held up her lips to me, smoothed her

hair again, and we went out of the room, she singing, and I almost beside myself.

In the next room she stopped for a moment and said to me in a low voice:

"It must seem strange to you that I am ready to take you at a moment's notice. Shall I tell you why? It is," she continued, taking my hand and placing it against her heart so that I could feel how rapidly and violently it palpitated; "it is because I shall not live as long as others, and I have promised myself to live more quickly."

"Don't speak to me like that, I entreat you."

"Oh, make yourself easy," she continued, laughing; "however short a time I have to live, I shall live longer than you will love me!"

And she went singing into the dining-room. ❧

CHAPTER II

Keeping Love

You are to me an object intensely desirable—the air I breathe in a room empty of you is unhealthy.
—John Keats

From Shakespearean sonnets to famous love letters through history, here you'll find readings and fun facts all about keeping love alive. Read about crushes turning to true love, and learn about how courtship has changed from ancient times through the Middle Ages and Renaissance all the way to the roaring twenties, swinging sixties, and beyond.

Catch a glimpse of historical figures letting down their guards as they write to their lovers, as you peruse love letters written by such famous historical figures as Napoleon, Oscar Wilde, Keats, and even a surprisingly romantic Abigail Adams! Then, put pen to paper and write your own love letter, which should be easier after you read some concrete suggestions on how best to express yourself.

You'll chuckle at the wise words from children on what love means, and enjoy several memoirs and stories from a variety of sources, from classic literature to current events. You'll also learn some of the more interesting traditions involving love and dating around the world. And don't miss the glossary of some very up-to-the-minute slang related to the endless dance of meeting, mating, and moving on.

Jane Austen Advises Her Niece on Matters of Love

Friday, Nov. 18, 1814.

I feel quite as doubtful as you could be, my dearest Fanny, as to when my letter may be finished, for I can command very little quiet time at present; but yet I must begin, for I know you will be glad to hear as soon as possible, and I really am impatient myself to be writing something on so very interesting a subject, though I have no hope of writing anything to the purpose. I shall do very little more, I dare say, than say over again what you have said before.

I was certainly a good deal surprised at first, as I had no suspicion of any change in your feelings, and I have no scruple in saying that you cannot be in love. My dear Fanny, I am ready to laugh at the idea, and yet it is no laughing matter to have had you so mistaken as to your own feelings. And with all my heart I wish I had cautioned you on that point when first you spoke to me; but, though I did not think you then so much in love, I did consider you as being attached in a degree quite sufficiently for happiness, as I had no doubt it would increase with opportunity, and from the time of our being in London together I thought you really very much in love. But you certainly are not at all—there is no concealing it.

What strange creatures we are! It seems as if your being secure of him had made you indifferent. There was a little disgust, I suspect, at the races, and I do not wonder at it. His expressions then would not do for one who had rather more acuteness, penetration, and taste, than love, which was your case. And yet, after all, I am surprised that the change in your feelings should be so great. He is just what he ever was, only more evidently and uniformly devoted to you. This is all the difference. How shall we account for it?

My dearest Fanny, I am writing what will not be of the smallest use to you. I am feeling differently every moment, and shall not be able to suggest a single thing that can assist your mind. I could lament in one sentence and laugh in the next, but as to opinion or counsel I am sure that none will be extracted worth having from this letter.

I read yours through the very evening I received it, getting away by myself. I could not bear to leave off when I had once begun. I was full of curiosity and concern. . . .

Poor dear Mr. A.! Oh, dear Fanny! Your mistake has been one that thousands of women fall into.

He was the first young man who attached himself to you. That was the charm, and most powerful it is. Among the multitudes, however, that make the same mistake with yourself, there can be few indeed who have so little reason to regret it; his character and his attachment leave you nothing to be ashamed of.

Upon the whole, what is to be done? You have no inclination for any other person. His situation in life, family, friends, and, above all, his character, his uncommonly amiable mind, strict principles, just notions, good habits, all that you know so well how to value, all that is really of the first importance, everything of this nature pleads his cause most strongly. You have no doubt of his having superior abilities, he has proved it at the University; he is, I dare say, such a scholar as your agreeable, idle brothers would ill bear a comparison with.

Oh, my dear Fanny! the more I write about him, the warmer my feelings become—the more strongly I feel the sterling worth of such a young man and the desirableness of your growing in love with him again. I recommend this most thoroughly. There are such beings in the world, perhaps one in a thousand, as the creature you and I should think perfection, where grace and spirit are united to worth, where the manners are equal to the heart and understanding, but such a person may not come in your way, or, if he does, he may not be the eldest son of a man of fortune, the near relation of your particular friend and belonging to your own county.

Think of all this, Fanny. Mr. A. has advantages which do not often meet in one person. His only fault, indeed, seems modesty. If he were less modest he would be more agreeable, speak louder, and look impudenter; and is not it a fine character of which modesty is the only defect? I have no doubt he will get more lively and more like yourselves as he is more with you; he will catch your ways if he belongs to you. And, as to there being any objection from his goodness, from the danger of his becoming even evangelical, I cannot admit that. I am by no means convinced that we ought not all to be evangelicals, and am at least persuaded that they who are so from reason and feeling must be happiest and safest. Do not be frightened from the connection by your brothers having most wit—wisdom is better than wit, and in the long run will certainly have the laugh on her side; and don't be frightened by the idea of his acting more strictly up to the precepts of the New Testament than others.

And now, my dear Fanny, having written so much on one side of the question, I shall turn round and entreat you not to commit yourself farther, and not to think of accepting him unless you really do like him. Anything is to be preferred or endured rather than marrying without affection; and if his deficiencies of manner, &c. &c., strike you more than all his good qualities, if you continue to think strongly of them, give him up at once. Things are now in such a state that you must resolve upon one or the other—either to allow him to go on as he has done, or whenever you are together behave with a coldness which may convince him that he has been deceiving himself. I have no doubt of his suffering a good deal for a time—a great deal when he feels that he must give you up; but it is no creed of mine, as you must be well aware, that such sort of disappointments kill anybody.

Yours very affectionately,
Jane Austen

COURTSHIP THROUGH WESTERN HISTORY

ANCIENT TIMES

According to legend, Antony and Cleopatra shared a passionate romantic love so deep it brought down an empire. As so often before and after, a statesman had to choose between allegiance to his state or to a mistress.

Ancient cultures had less of a stigma attached to homosexual affairs than the eras that followed, and it was not unusual for young men to form close attachments outside their more traditional heterosexual marriages.

MIDDLE AGES

In medieval times, suitors followed the highly formal rules and rituals of courtly love. As a model, they based their courtship on the stories played out by the lovelorn characters they saw on stage and in verse, wooing their intendeds with flowery poetry and serenades. Think Shakespeare, Marlowe, or Bacon. The most highly regarded virtues were chastity and honor, so in order to be worthy of love, men knew they must act nobly, and with great chivalry. And in order to deserve this chivalry, the object of his affection knew she had to keep herself pure and true always.

THE RENAISSANCE

Courtly love continued to be a formal affair, with rules and social conventions governing all interaction between the sexes. Much of the poetry and art of the period celebrates an ideal of romantic love.

THE PURITANS

In colonial America, as in Europe, it was standard for parents to exercise great control over their children's courtships and marriages. As it had been since time began, marriage had more to do with the property arrangement between two families than with romance and love. Usually, several letters and discussions would take place between prospective in-laws before even informing the soon-to-be bride and groom of their upcoming nuptials.

VICTORIAN TIMES

In the Victorian era, courtship remained very formal. Couples smitten with desire rarely saw each other without the presence of a chaperone, and marriage proposals were frequently written. There were rules for everything, ranging from what constituted a proper introduction to elaborate rules about walking together, such as the distance between a walking couple had to be such "that a dog might pass between them."

THE ROARING TWENTIES

Youth culture was invented in the twenties, and parents everywhere were scandalized at the thought of their children dating. Maybe even necking in automobiles! In fact, the rise in the popularity of cars meant that courting moved from porch swings to back seats, and young women shamed their parents by such acts as shortening their hemlines, smoking cigarettes in public, and bobbing their hair.

THE SWINGING SIXTIES

The era of "Free Love" saw the pendulum swing about as far from Victorian times as possible. Any formality was out, and "letting it all hang out" was in. Gone were the rules and gender roles of yesteryear, and romance took a back seat to pure hedonism. The only rule for dating was that there were no rules. In fact, even the term "dating" fell out of favor, as couples "hooked up" and then swapped partners with casual abandon.

MODERN-DAY ROMANCE

And so we've come to the present day, where the influence of the permissive '60s is still felt, but on the other hand, bestselling authors advise men and women to return to the restrictive social codes of days gone by. While we have no formal rules for dating, there has been a return to a more traditional view of courtship, and modern men and women are learning once again to appreciate the art of a well-turned phrase (in email, perhaps!) and the delicious pleasures of just plain flirting.

Sonnet CXXX

BY WILLIAM SHAKESPEARE

My mistress' eyes are nothing like the sun;
Coral is far more red than her lips' red;
If snow be white, why then her breasts are dun;
If hairs be wires, black wires grow on her head.
I have seen roses damasked, red and white,
But no such roses see I in her cheeks,

And in some perfumes is there more delight
Than in the breath that from my mistress reeks.
I love to hear her speak, yet well I know
That music hath a far more pleasing sound.
I grant I never saw a goddess go;
My mistress when she walks treads on the
    ground.
    And yet, by heaven, I think my love as rare
    As any she belied with false compare.

My Life in Crushes: True Tales
BY KAREN STEIGER

SLAPPY MCGOO: THE FIRST GREAT LOVE

What Attracted Me to Him in the First Place:
Intense, slightly maniac, dark brown eyes that never blinked in a staring contest.

Nothing turns me on like a boy who runs hot and cold, hot and cold. You want me to crush on you? Then be my best friend one minute, and a haughty stranger the next. There were moonlit summer nights when I walked him back home from—oh God—Catholic youth group meetings (those faith-based teenage breeding grounds), and he would rattle off a list of approximately thirteen other girls who were tormenting him to the deepest core of his soul, and as I walked back home alone, I thought, "Oh, wow, he's confiding in me," even though it hurt to imagine that I was probably—at the most optimistic estimate—#14 on that list.

Why It Didn't Work:
Mutual lack of self-esteem. He couldn't tell me what he needed to tell me before I jumped both feet first into a Permanent Relationship. It was too late then, anyway. I loved him so much that when he was concerned that one of the 32,634 Official Loves of His Life would see me with him at the parish carnival, I volunteered to play the role of a second or third cousin. Joined a frat in college.

Why Slappy McGoo Will Always Have a Special Place in My Heart:

Although I had had less important, less emotionally draining crushes beforehand, Slappy was my first taste of love, the kind of love that is set to Aerosmith ballads.

TALKING STICK PONY:
THE FIRST OFFICIAL BOYFRIEND

What Attracted Me to Him in the First Place:
Was the funniest and most subversive person at the Catholic youth weekend retreat.

Looked exactly like Jonathan Silverman in *Brighton Beach Memoirs*. Was moderately interested in dating me.

Why It Didn't Work:
Our first official date took place at an elaborate Passion play at scary evangelical church. Our first kiss took place during a showing of the thirtysomething nostalgia fest, *Indian Summer*.

His friend felt the need to call me every day (managing to call me more often than Talking Stick Pony himself, incidentally) and effectively killed our relationship by informing me what Talking Stick Pony really thought of me: "Well, he says that you're not the best-looking, but then he says he isn't either."

Why Talking Stick Pony Will Always Have a Special Place in My Heart:
Was responsible for a couple of big firsts—first official boyfriend, first kiss. Breakup was amiable.

RAW CARROTS TURPITUDE:
THE BESTEST FRIEND

What Attracted Me to Him in the First Place:
Adorable features and very soft floppy brown hair; talented in arts and drama; frightening-

ly intelligent; the funniest person I have ever met.

The only other person I had ever met who had seen and enjoyed *The Adventures of Baron Munchausen,* one of my very, very favorite movies.

Why It Didn't Work:

He took everyone in the whole wide world to a formal dance except me.

Why Raw Carrots Turpitude Will Always Have a Special Place in My Heart:

Is still my bestest friend whom I couldn't even imagine living without. Still has adorable features and very soft (if shorter) brown hair. Remains talented in arts and drama. Is to this day frighteningly intelligent and the funniest person I have ever met. Also likes boys. So that wound up working out really well, actually.

PORKCHOP W. FLAPJACK: THE KEEPER

What Attracted Me to Him in the First Place:
Sexy, sexy muscular legs and lovely light green eyes. Had an aura of danger with his shaved head and goatee. Also carried a condom in his wallet. (Gasp!) He was one of those boys.

Why It Worked:
Thoroughly corrupted me in just about every way within four months. I was instantly adopted by his wonderful, functional family. He's nice to my mom and brother and grandma.

Why Porkchop W. Flapjack Will Always Have a Special Place in My Heart:
He was my first taste of love—the good, recip-

rocal kind that makes you happy when you think about it and that doesn't waver no matter how long you're together. We've got a good shot at that "happily ever after" thing.

> *For the full story on these crushes, visit www.nopretension.com.*

To His Coy Mistress
BY ANDREW MARVELL

Had we but world enough, and time,
This coyness, lady, were no crime.
We would sit down and think which way
To walk, and pass our long love's day;
Thou by the Indian Ganges' side
Shouldst rubies find; I by the tide
Of Humber would complain. I would
Love you ten years before the Flood;
And you should, if you please, refuse
Till the conversion of the Jews.
My vegetable love should grow
Vaster than empires, and more slow.
An hundred years should go to praise
Thine eyes, and on thy forehead gaze;
Two hundred to adore each breast,

But thirty thousand to the rest;
An age at least to every part,
And the last age should show your heart.
For, lady, you deserve this state,
Nor would I love at lower rate.

But at my back I always hear
Time's winged chariot hurrying near;
And yonder all before us lie
Deserts of vast eternity.
Thy beauty shall no more be found,
Nor, in thy marble vault, shall sound
My echoing song; then worms shall try
That long preserv'd virginity,
And your quaint honour turn to dust,
And into ashes all my lust.
The grave's a fine and private place,
But none I think do there embrace.

Now therefore, while the youthful hue
Sits on thy skin like morning dew,
And while thy willing soul transpires
At every pore with instant fires,
Now let us sport us while we may;
And now, like am'rous birds of prey,
Rather at once our time devour,
Than languish in his slow-chapp'd power.
Let us roll all our strength, and all
Our sweetness, up into one ball;
And tear our pleasures with rough strife
Thorough the iron gates of life.
Thus, though we cannot make our sun
Stand still, yet we will make him run.

Love Letters
Through History

KING HENRY VIII TO ANNE BOLEYN

King Henry VIII (1491–1547) is probably the most famous Tudor king of England—though not for his writing. His six marriages in the quest for a son will forever brand him as a cruel husband, but this letter, to wife number two (perhaps the only one he truly loved, though he had her beheaded after she gave birth to a daughter), shows a softer side of the brute.

c. 1528

In debating with myself the contents of your letters I have been put to great agony; not knowing how to understand them, whether to my disadvantage as shown in some places, or to my advantage in others. I beseech you now with all my heart defi-

nitely to let me know your whole mind as to the love between us; for necessity compels me to plague you for a reply, having been for more than a year now struck by the dart of love, and being uncertain either of failure or of finding a place in your heart and affection, which point has certainly kept me for some time from naming you my mistress, since if you only love me with an ordinary love the name is not appropriate to you, seeing that it stands for an uncommon position very remote from the ordinary; but if it pleases you to do the duty of a true, loyal mistress and friend, and to give yourself body and heart to me, who have been, and will be, your very loyal servant (if your rigour does not forbid me), I promise you that not only the name will be due to you, but also to take you as my sole mistress, casting off all others than yourself out of mind and affection, and to serve you only; begging

*you to make me a complete reply to this my rude
letter as to how far and in what I can trust; and if
it does not please you to reply in writing, to let me
know of some place where I can have it by word of
mouth, the which place I will seek out with all my
heart. No more for fear of wearying you. Written by
the hand of him who would willingly remain your*

HR

OSCAR WILDE TO LORD ALFRED DOUGLAS

**Oscar Wilde (1854–1900), famous poet, novelist,
and playwright of the nineteenth century, is well-
known for his turn of phrase and biting wit. These
letters show a softer, more romantic side of him.
Unfortunately, they also led indirectly to his arrest
and trial for the "crime" of being homosexual.**

c. 1891

My own dear boy—Your sonnet is quite lovely and it is a marvel that those red roseleaf lips of yours should have been made no less for the music of song than for the madness of kissing. Your slim gilt soul walks between passion and poetry. I know that Hyacinthus, whom Apollo loved so madly, was you in Greek days. Why are you alone in London, and when do you go to Salisbury? Do go there to cool your hands in the grey twilight of Gothic things, and come here whenever you like. It is a lovely place—it only lacks you; but go to Salisbury first. Always with undying love,

Yours,
Oscar

NAPOLEON BONAPARTE
TO JOSEPHINE BEAUHARNAIS

Napoleon Bonaparte (1763–1821) was not only a feared and celebrated military man, but was also a tender lover, known for his prolific letter-writing. In fact, rumor has it that he wrote as many as 75,000 letters over the course of his lifetime! Many of these letters were to his beloved bride Josephine, including this letter, written just prior to their 1796 wedding.

Paris, December 1795

I wake filled with thoughts of you. Your portrait and the intoxicating evening which we spent yesterday have left my senses in turmoil. Sweet, incomparable Josephine, what a strange effect you have on my heart! Are you angry? Do I see you looking sad? Are you worried? . . . My soul aches with sorrow, and there can be no rest for you lover; but is there still more in store for me when, yielding to the pro-

found feelings which overwhelm me, I draw from
your lips, from your heart a love which consumes
me with fire? Ah! it was last night that I fully real-
ized how false an image of you your portrait gives!
You are leaving at noon; I shall see you in three
hours.

Until then, mio dolce amor, a thousand kisses; but
give me none in return, for they set my blood on fire.

OLIVER CROMWELL
TO ELIZABETH CROMWELL

**Oliver Cromwell (1599–1658) led an English rebellion
that deposed and executed King Charles I in 1649. He
united the kingdoms of England, Scotland, and
Wales, and ruled them until his death. Throughout
his life, he remained deeply in love with his wife
Elizabeth, whom he had married in 1620 at the age
of twenty-one.**

Dunbar, 4 September 1650

For my beloved Wife Elizabeth Cromwell, at the Cockpit:

My Dearest,

I have not leisure to write much, but I could chide thee that in many of thy letters thou writest to me, that I should not be unmindful of thee and thy little ones. Truly, if I love thee not too well, I think I err not on the other hand much. Thou art dearer to me than any creature; let that suffice.

The Lord hath showed us an exceeding mercy: who can tell how great it is. My weak faith hath been upheld. I have been in my inward man marvellously supported; though I assure thee, I grow an old man, and feel infirmities of age marvellously stealing upon me. Would my corruptions did as fast decrease. Pray on my behalf in the latter respect. The particulars of our late success Harry Vane or Gil Pickering will impart to thee. My love to all dear friends. I rest thine,

Oliver Cromwell

JOHN KEATS TO FANNY BRAWNE

John Keats (1795–1821) was a leading poet of the nineteenth century, writing such famous poems as "Ode on a Grecian Urn" and the epic poem, "Hyperion," during his short life. The true story of John Keats and Fanny Brawne reads like something a poet would invent: Young poet meets girl and falls instantly in love with her. They become secretly engaged, only his health fails and he leaves her to go recuperate in Italy. Alas, instead of being cured, he dies there in 1821 at the age of twenty-five, and is buried with one of her unopened letters in his coffin.

Wednesday morning. (Kentish Town, 1820)

My Dearest Girl,

I have been a walk this morning with a book in my hand, but as usual I have been occupied with nothing but you: I wish I could say in an agreeable manner. I am tormented day and night. They talk of my going to Italy. 'Tis certain I shall never recover if I am to be so long separate from you: yet with all this devotion to you I cannot persuade myself into any confidence of you. . . .

You are to me an object intensely desirable—the air I breathe in a room empty of you is unhealthy. I am not the same to you—no—you can wait—you have a thousand activities—you can be happy without me. Any party, anything to fill up the day has been enough.

How have you pass'd this month? Who have you smil'd with? All this may seem savage in me. You do no feel as I do—you do not know what it is to love—one day you may—your time is not come . . .

I cannot live without you, and not only you but chaste you; virtuous you. The Sun rises and sets, the day passes, and you follow the bent of your inclination to a certain extent—you have no conception of the quantity of miserable feeling that passes through me in a day—Be serious! Love is not a plaything—and again do not write unless you can do it with a crystal conscience. I would sooner die for want of you than—

Yours for ever, J. Keats

LORD BYRON TO TERESA GUICCIOLI

Lord Byron (1788–1824) was one of England's most notorious womanizers. After his wife left him, he spent the years 1818–23 with Teresa Guiccioli. Filled with a desire to help Greece obtain independence from Turkey, he joined their fight in December 1823, but died of fever less than a year later.

25 August 1819

My dearest Teresa,

I have read this book in your garden;—my love, you were absent, or else I could not have read it. It is a favourite book of yours, and the writer was a friend of mine. You will not understand these English words, and others will not understand them,—which is the reason I have not scrawled them in Italian. But you will recognize the handwriting of him who passionately loved you, and you will divine that, over a book which was yours, he could only think of love.

In that word, beautiful in all languages, but most so in yours—Amor mio—is comprised my existence here and hereafter. I feel I exist here, and I feel I shall exist hereafter,—to what purpose you will decide; my destiny rests with you, and you are a woman, eighteen years of age, and two out of a convent. I love you, and you love me,—at least, you say so, and act as if you did so, which last is a great consolation in all events.

But I more than love you, and cannot cease to love you. Think of me, sometimes, when the Alps and ocean divide us, but they never will, unless you wish it.

ABIGAIL ADAMS TO JOHN ADAMS

John Adams (1735–1826), the second president of the United States, married his wife, Abigail, in 1764, and their correspondence is a testament to the love and happiness they shared during their 54 years together.

23 December 1792

John, my dearest friend,

Should I draw you a picture of my heart it would be what I hope you would still love though it contained nothing new. The early possession you obtained there, and the absolute power you have obtained over it, leaves not the smallest space unoccupied. I look back to the early days of our acquaintance and friendship to the days of love and innocence, and, with indescribable pleasure, I have seen near a score of years roll over our heads

*with an affection heightened and improved by
time, nor have the dreary years of absence in the
smallest degree effaced from my mind the image of
the dear untitled man to whom I gave my heart.*

Abigail

Sonnet LXXI

BY WILLIAM SHAKESPEARE

*No longer mourn for me when I am dead
Than you shall hear the surly sullen bell
Give warning to the World that I am fled
From this vile world with vilest worms to dwell.
Nay, if you read this line, remember not
The hand that writ it, for I love you so*

That I in your sweet thoughts would be forgot,
If thinking on me then should make you woe.
O, if, I say, you look upon this verse,
When I, perhaps, compounded am with clay,
Do not so much as my poor name rehearse,
But let your love even with my life decay,
　　Lest the wise world should look into your
　　moan,
　　And mock you with me after I am gone.

WRITING THE PERFECT LOVE LETTER

In a world where email is ubiquitous, and the longest thing you write by hand could fit on a sticky note, the art of writing love letters seems to be dying. But nothing can take the place of an actual paper envelope, perhaps even sealed with old-fashioned wax. All the emails in the world won't have the impact of one carefully penned missive—not to mention the fact that emails don't lend themselves to being tied up with pretty ribbon and saved for future perusal.

For the letter-writer, the simple act of forming thoughts and writing them down can be a pleasure. And for the lucky recipient, anticipation is part of the fun: Imagine carefully opening an envelope to reveal a hand-written letter or card filled with sentimental language proclaiming love. Forthwith, some tips and tricks to make writing a love letter a breeze.

Know your audience.
Is this letter going to someone you just started dating, or to your companion of the last ten years? In a new relationship, there is always a danger of over-emoting, so be sure to write

from the heart in a tone that will warm the heart of the reader, not make him (or her) worry that you're a stalker!

Size isn't everything.

There is something wonderful about a short, sweet note. If you can keep yourself to a page or two, that's generally better than a twenty-page novella. On the other hand, keep the previous advice in mind. If your lover is the sort to enjoy a long, intricate letter that takes an hour to read, follow your instinct. But if you're not sure, remember that brevity is often called the soul of wit.

Don't be afraid of sentiment.

In a love letter, it's time to set aside the modern penchant for irony. Embrace your inner earnest self, the voice you usually avoid as too sentimental. Tell the person you love how you feel. Say "I love you" and mean it.

Use specifics.

Do you especially love the smell of your beloved's hair? Is there a funny little laugh he has that drives you wild? Do you often think back to some random date you had, and remember what she was wearing? The more specific things you mention, the more personal it feels to the recipient. Don't be generic. Mention the little stuff.

When in doubt, throw in a quote.

This book and others are filled with wonderful quotes and aphorisms about love and romance. A snippet of poetry, a dash of Shakespeare—these are the things that add class to a love letter.

The letter itself should be on fine stationery or an especially lovely blank card. Because how it looks is important, it's best to write a draft of the letter on scrap paper, and only when you are sure it is done should you copy it carefully on the actual card or paper.

If you follow these tips, and write from your heart, you will delight your lover with a special letter that he or she will treasure forever.

Sonnet XVIII

BY WILLIAM SHAKESPEARE

Shall I compare thee to a summer's day?
Thou art more lovely and more temperate.
Rough winds do shake the darling buds of May,
And summer's lease hath all too short a date.
Sometime too hot the eye of heaven shines,
And often is his gold complexion dimmed;

And every fair from fair sometime declines,
By chance, or nature's changing course,
   untrimmed
But thy eternal summer shall not fade,
Nor lose possession of that fair thou ow'st,
Nor shall Death brag thou wand'rest in his
   shade,
When in eternal lines to time thou grow'st.
   So long as men can breathe or eyes can see,
   So long lives this, and this gives life to thee. 🌹

One Night

BY CONSTANTINE CAVAFY

The room was cheap and sordid,
hidden above the suspect taverna.
From the window you could see the alley,
dirty and narrow. From below

came the voices of workmen
playing cards, enjoying themselves.

And there on that ordinary, plain bed
I had love's body, knew those intoxicating lips,
red and sensual,
red lips so intoxicating
that now as I write, after so many years,
in my lonely house, I'm drunk with passion
again. 🌸

DATING ADVICE FROM THE YOUNGER SET

Questions concerning love and dating were posed to a group of children, aged five to ten:

What do most people do on a date?

"On the first date, they just tell each other lies, and that usually gets them interested enough to go for a second date." (Tim, 10)

When is it okay to kiss someone?

"You should never kiss a girl unless you have enough bucks to buy her a big ring and her own video player, 'cause she'll want to have videos of the wedding." (Rob, 10)

"Never kiss in front of other people. It's a big embarrassing thing if anybody sees you. But if nobody sees you, I might be willing to try it with a handsome boy, but just for a few hours." (Tamara, 9)

"It's never okay to kiss a boy. They always slobber all over you. That's why I stopped doing it." (Anne, 10)

Concerning why love happens between two people:

"No one is sure why it happens, but I heard

it has something to do with how you smell. That's why perfume and deodorant are so popular." (Isabella, 9)

"I think you're supposed to get shot with an arrow or something, but the rest of it isn't supposed to be so painful." (Thor, 8)

On what falling in love is like:

"Like an avalanche where you have to run for your life." (Roger, 9)

"If falling in love is anything like learning multiplication tables, I don't want to do it. It takes too long to learn." (Louie, 7)

On the role of good looks in love and romance:

"If you want to be loved by somebody who isn't already in your family, it doesn't hurt to be beautiful." (Joanne, 8)

"It isn't always just how you look. Look at me. I'm handsome like anything and I haven't got anybody to marry me yet." (Gary, 7)

"Beauty is skin deep. But how rich you are can last a long time." (Penelope, 9)

Concerning why lovers often hold hands:

"They want to make sure their rings don't fall off, because they paid good money for them." (Allen, 8)

Confidential opinions about love:

"I'm in favor of love as long as it doesn't happen when *The Simpsons* are on TV." (Chrissie, 6)

"Love will find you, even if you are trying to hide from it. I've been trying to hide from it since I was five, but the girls keep finding me." (Bart, 8)

Personal qualities necessary to be a good lover:

"One of you should know how to write a check. Because, even if you have tons of love, there is still going to be a lot of bills." (Evie, 8)

Some surefire ways to make a person fall in love with you:

"Tell them you own a whole bunch of candy stores." (David, 6)

"Don't do things like have smelly, green sneakers. You might get attention, but attention ain't the same thing as love." (Roberto, 9)

"One way is to take the girl out to eat. Make sure it's something she likes to eat. French fries usually work for me." (Sam 9)

How can you tell if two adults eating dinner at a restaurant are in love?

"Just see if the man pays the check. That's how you can tell if he's in love." (Aaron, 9)

"Lovers will just be staring at each other and their food will get cold. Other people care more about the food." (Joey, 8)

"It's love if they order one of those desserts that are on fire. They like to order those because it's just like their hearts are on fire." (Suzanne, 9)

What most people are thinking when they say "I love you":

"The person is thinking: Yeah, I really do love him, but I hope he showers at least once a day." (Brandon, 9)

How a person learns to kiss:

"You learn it right on the spot, when the gushy feelings get the best of you." (Gary, 7)

"It might help if you watched soap operas all day." (Kelly, 9)

How to make love endure:

"Spend most of your time loving instead of going to work." (Tom, 7)

"Don't forget your wife's name. That will mess up the love." (George, 8)

"Be a good kisser. It might make your wife forget that you never take the trash out." (Howard, 8)

Geek Courtship: The Early Days (A True Story, Sadly Enough)

I was seven years old. His name was Harvey, and he lived in the house directly across the street.

Harvey was a geek, no doubt about it. I think of him from the vantage point of all the years gone, and I see a boy with ugly horn-rimmed glasses all dressed in brown, his hair parted haphazardly to one side, springing up awkwardly from his head. God knows why I latched onto him. He was older—nine—and made it clear from the moment our moms introduced us to each other, waiting for us to do or say something cute (after all, that's your job when you're a kid, right?), that he wanted nothing to do with girls, and even less to do with me in particular. Naturally, I fell in love with him right then.

I didn't really see much of Harvey. He was a few grades ahead of me in school, and in the afternoon, he never played outside with the other kids in the neighborhood. I don't think he even rode the school bus. Oh, how was I going to get him to notice me?

"Mommy, can I have some of the wood that's left over from the bookshelf Daddy built?" My parents always encouraged me in whatever creative endeavor I had going, and I guess my mother assumed I was going to bang some nails into wood and call it a project. Really, it was easy. I found a flat piece of wood, nailed a two-by-four to it, and I was done. All that was left to do was grab a big marker and write in letters a foot high: I LOVE HARVEY. I knew that the next day, Harvey would walk out of his front door directly across the street, see my sign, and know I loved him, at which point he would of course start loving me back. With a few taps of the hammer, the sign was firmly anchored in the front lawn, for all the world to see. Especially Harvey.

Nothing happened the next day. Or the next. My sign was tilting over to one side. It had rained overnight and the letters were dripping. I guess I realized at that point that it wasn't going to work. Maybe the letters weren't big enough? On the third day, I pulled the sign up, and threw the wood back in the garage. That's it. I don't remember the rest of the story, except that we moved away a year later, and I never saw Harvey again.

—M.Z.

John Evereldown
BY EDWIN ARLINGTON ROBINSON

Where are you going to-night, to-night,—
Where are you going, John Evereldown?
There's never the sign of a star in sight,
Nor a lamp that's nearer than Tilbury Town.
Why do you stare as a dead man might?
Where are you pointing away from the light?
And where are you going to-night, to-night,—
Where are you going, John Evereldown?

Right through the forest, where none can see,
There's where I'm going, to Tilbury Town.
The men are asleep,—or awake, may be,—
But the women are calling John Evereldown.
Ever and ever they call for me,
And while they call can a man be free?

*So right through the forest, where none can
    see,*
There's where I'm going, to Tilbury Town.

But why are you going so late, so late,—
Why are you going, John Evereldown?
*Though the road be smooth and the way be
    straight,*
There are two long leagues to Tilbury Town.
Come in by the fire, old man, and wait!
Why do you chatter out there by the gate?
And why are you going so late, so late,—
Why are you going, John Evereldown?

I follow the women wherever they call,—
That's why I'm going to Tilbury Town.
God knows if I pray to be done with it all,
But God is no friend to John Evereldown.

So the clouds may come and the rain may fall,
The shadows may creep and the dead men
   crawl,—
But I follow the women wherever they call,
And that's why I'm going to Tilbury Town. 🌹

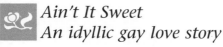

Ain't It Sweet
An idyllic gay love story
BY DONALD CURRIE

How do you talk about happiness without dribbling away into saggy slipshod clichés? There are moments in life, rare indeed and fleeting as a mirage, when all the hopeless dreams you carry on your weary back like a derelict's knapsack suddenly burgeon into wondrous life and bless you with a blissful interlude of simple joy.

When Jeremy and I met in the early '70s we were both in the springtime of our lives and God was gracious enough to get us going on an April afternoon on a Big Sur hillside, glistening Ireland green after a long winter drenching, popping and crackling with a firework display of wildflowers and butterflies. We romped and stomped and tumbled about on those luscious meadows soaring up out of the sea, our hearts brimming with young manhood and hopped up with blossoming love.

Disney couldn't have done it better, and we had real genitals, me and my little pony. It was splendor in the grass beneath a big billowing sky, our dervish dance of desire, and we fell right now in love before we even knew each other and it took, and it stayed, and it lasted five years. Not bad for a roll of the dice from a roll in the hay. And before you could say "what was your name again?" we had moved into a gardener's cottage at the back of the backyard of a ramshackle beyond Marin and set up house, two willowy lads enmeshed in each others' lusts and longings, bonking like Energizer bunnies and decorating our rickety shed with old thrift-store gimcracks and Dumpster throw-aways.

We painted the walls and ceiling pale sky blue, a rusted metal bed frame iridescent gold, and found a Jean Harlow-like dresser made of beveled mirrors with soft lights emanating from within it to shimmer in the corner of our backyard boudoir. Then we loaded the place down with bookshelves and settled in, with a little black-and-white puppy named Sheba and a big black-and-white cat named Irma and a single lovebird we christened Madame Bovary. And there we nested with our scampering trilling menagerie in our picture perfect setting, all too precious, like a Thomas Kinkade painting but with a lot of sex, legs in the air on the golden bed, cries of joy flung up to heaven by the shimmering light of the silvery dressing table.

Jeremy was a doting and faithful mate. Children and dogs adored him and so did I. He was enamored of my farouche artiste airs and I of his "man of few words" reliability, which seemed to cover a depth of sensitivity and a cauldron of hot male mystery. He found in me the perfectly pliable lover, ever ready at the drop of trou to swoon and make much of his big fat buddy, but more importantly, I was most definitely the fem in the affair and this let him feel both manly and sensitive. He had to have his boylove time at this time in his evolving manhood but only with a boy of some sexual ambiguity and I fit that bill real neat, like a perfect '70s unisex haircut. I was lissome and sensitive and pretty helpless when it came to the butchy things in life, car repair, heavy machinery, that lot, and Jeremy was a regular Budweiser ad for such things as power tools and holding down a job. He pretty much took care of the both of us, getting odd jobs in gardening and construction work while I stayed home and read through the Western canon, fixed dinner, and got ready to be pounced upon when he came home all greasy and sweaty, still wearing his work belt, throwing me onto the kitchen table and slamming me in a porno frenzy while the lasagna bubbled in the oven.

It was damn sweet and could have gone on

forever if we both hadn't gotten restless for change and I made the first mistake of joining a gym, just as Nautilus machines were invented and went from lanky and ladylike to pumped up and make-believe hunky at the same time as he started sniffing around for girls. But this schism was a ways away and in the beginning we reveled in our gayboy Garden of Eden and put down deep clinging roots. I'd say we had two years of perfect bliss followed by three years of a slow diminuendo as we changed in all the wrong ways before each other's disillusioned eyes, a sad and bittersweet parting in Athens—of all perfect places—a year's separation while he traveled around the world and sent back pictures of himself in Hindu headgear and Thai sarongs and I moved back to San Francisco to become a Castro clone and bed everything that moved.

Truth is, though we both clung to each other in our happy-go-lucky home we were really rolling stones, perpetual adolescents, who always thought something more exotic or life-changing was waiting for us just around the corner. And truth also is that though he'd found his myth of bonded brotherhood in me, he was really searching, in spite of his wanderlust, for the more typical scenario of wife and kids, and buttboy and beagle just didn't fulfill it.

I guess I have the proud distinction of having been his only boy lover, as before and after me he was a ladies' man, plain and simple. What prompted him to stroll down my boulevard for those brief years is anybody's guess. He was a shut-down locked-up guy and did what he did for reasons unexplained, but for our time together we were entangled in each other's dreams as if we'd been born to nestle and rest in a cradle of peace, endlessly rocking, and our love was luminous and true, gentle, sexy, and palsy-walsy perfect. And if it eventually evaporated, truth is all things do, nothing lasts, it is all lost, even I who speak and you who listen, and it is all, in the end, ineffable. ❧

Donald Currie's award-winning CD, Sex and Mayhem Part I, *about growing up gay in the '50s and '60s, prompted* Echo Magazine *to call him "a gay Holden Caulfield." His work is available at www.cdbaby.com/cd/ donaldcurrie.*

I Loved You First

BY CHRISTINA ROSSETTI

I loved you first: but afterwards your love
Outsoaring mine, sang such a loftier song
As drowned the friendly cooings of my dove.
Which owes the other most? my love was long,
And yours one moment seemed to wax more
*   strong;*
I loved and guessed at you, you construed me
And loved me for what might or might not be—
Nay, weights and measurements do us both
*   wrong.*
For verily love knows not 'mine' or 'thine',
With separate 'I' and 'thou' free love has done,
For one is both and both are one in love.
Rich love knows naught of 'thine that is not
*   mine',*

Both have the strength and both the length
thereof,
Both of us, of the love which makes us one.

ॐ

COURTSHIP AROUND THE GLOBE

AFRICA

The Surma people of Ethiopia practice a violent courtship ritual: Every year, after the harvest is over, hundreds of Surma men come together and stage wild and violent stick fights. The victors win the hearts of prospective wives.

The Wodaabe nomad men of Niger spend hours preening and painting themselves for an all-male beauty contest. The women act as judges and select their husbands and lovers.

EUROPE

The tiny country of Luxembourg is home to a charming courtship tradition. The fourth Sunday of Lent is known as Bretzelsonndeg (Pretzel Sunday). A man is required to bake a specially decorated pretzel-shaped cake and deliver it to a woman he is interested in. If she is likewise interested, three weeks later (on Easter Sunday) she responds with a gift of a decorated egg. Custom dictates that the larger and more ornate the pretzel cake was, the more effort she must put into her gift of sweets and a decorated egg.

In Sicily, young unmarried lovers exchange rings to indicate an "engagement" even when there is no intention of getting married. These long faux engagements—which often end amicably when the relationship has run its course—are called *fidanzamenti*, and help preserve decorum with older, more traditional relatives who may not approve of long romantic liaisons that don't involve marriage. The lovers wear *fedinas*, which are similar to wedding bands but thinner and less expensive.

In the Ukraine, flowers play an important role in courtship. A single rose is appropriate for a first date, and showing up without flowers at all is frowned upon.

ASIA

Many marriage rituals in Japan help add mystery to the service, and traditional ceremonies call for decorative costumes and actions. For example, some couples believe that using a fog machine during the wedding ceremony will add a sense of secrecy by hiding the bride and groom from onlookers.

In Japan, the average age for women to marry is 25. In fact, an unmarried woman in her late twenties may be referred to by the derogatory term "Christmas Cake," which is an allusion to the fact that after December 25, the value of a prized holiday cake goes down quickly.

In India, traditional marriage is still arranged by parents. Weddings are times of great celebration, expense, and feasting. In a traditional ceremony, the bride and groom exchange garlands before circling around a fire three times.

Song to Celia
BY BEN JONSON

Drink to me only with thine eyes,
And I will pledge with mine;
Or leave a kiss but in the cup,
And I'll not look for wine.
The thirst that from the soul doth rise
Doth ask a drink divine;
But might I of Jove's nectar sup,
I would not change for thine.

I sent thee late a rosy wreath,
Not so much honouring thee
As giving it a hope, that there
It could not withered be.
But thou thereon didst only breathe,
And sent'st it back to me;
Since when it grows, and smells, I swear,
Not of itself, but thee.

Jane Eyre
BY CHARLOTTE BRONTË

In this scene near the end of the novel, Jane has returned to Mr. Rochester, unable to forget him. She had left some time ago, after their wedding was cancelled when it turned out he had a crazy wife living secretly in the attic. But now that the wife has perished in a fire—a tragedy which also disfigured and blinded Rochester himself—Jane has returned, unbeknownst to him, to declare her undying love.

"Can there be life here?" I asked.

Yes, life of some kind there was; for I heard a movement—that narrow front-door was unclosing, and some shape was about to issue from the grange.

It opened slowly: a figure came out into the twilight and stood on the step; a man without a hat: he stretched forth his hand as if to feel whether it rained. Dusk as it was, I had recognised him—it was my master, Edward Fairfax Rochester, and no other.

I stayed my step, almost my breath, and stood to watch him—to examine him, myself unseen, and alas! to him invisible. It was a sudden meeting, and one in which rapture was kept well in check by pain. I had no difficulty in restraining my voice from exclamation, my step from hasty advance.

His form was of the same strong and stalwart contour as ever: his port was still erect, his hair was still raven black; nor were his features altered or sunk: not in one year's space, by any sorrow, could his athletic strength be quelled or his vigorous prime blighted. But in his countenance I saw a change: that looked desperate and brooding—that reminded me of some wronged and fettered wild beast or bird, dangerous to approach in his sullen woe. The caged eagle, whose gold-ringed eyes cruelty has extinguished, might look as looked that sightless Samson.

And, reader, do you think I feared him in his blind ferocity?—if you do, you little know me. A soft hope blest with my sorrow that soon I should dare to drop a kiss on that brow of rock, and on those lips so sternly sealed beneath it: but not yet. I would not accost him yet.

He descended the one step, and advanced slowly and gropingly towards the grass-plat. Where was his daring stride now? Then he paused, as if he knew not which way to turn. He lifted his hand and opened his eyelids; gazed blank, and with a straining effort, on the sky, and toward the amphitheatre of trees: one saw that all to him was void darkness. He stretched his right hand (the left arm, the mutilated one, he kept hidden in his bosom); he seemed to wish by touch to gain an idea of what lay around him: he met but vacancy still; for the trees were some yards off where he stood. He relinquished the endeavor, folded his arms, and stood quiet and mute in the rain, now falling fast on his uncovered head. At this moment John approached him from some quarter.

"Will you take my arm, sir?" he said; "there is a heavy shower coming on: had you not better go in?"

"Let me alone," was the answer.

John withdrew without having observed me. Mr. Rochester now tried to walk about: vainly,—all was too uncertain. He groped his way back to the house, and, re-entering it, closed the door.

I now drew near and knocked: John's wife opened for me. "Mary," I said, "how are you?"

She started as if she had seen a ghost: I calmed her. To her hurried "Is it really you, miss, come at this late hour to this lonely place?" I answered by taking her hand; and then I followed her into the kitchen, where John now sat by a good fire. I explained to them, in few words, that I had heard all which had happened since I left Thornfield, and that I was come to see Mr. Rochester. I asked John to go down to the turn-pike-house, where I had dismissed the chaise, and bring my trunk, which I had left there: and then, while I removed my bonnet and shawl, I questioned Mary as to whether I could be accommodated at the Manor House for the night; and finding that arrangements to that effect, though difficult, would not be impossible, I informed her I should stay. Just at this moment the parlor-bell rang.

"When you go in," said I, "tell your master that a person wishes to speak to him, but do not give my name."

"I don't think he will see you," she answered; "he refuses everybody."

When she returned, I inquired what he had said. "You are to send in your name and your business," she replied. She then proceeded to fill a glass with water, and place it on a tray, together with candles.

"Is that what he rang for?" I asked.

"Yes: he always has candles brought in at dark, though he is blind."

"Give the tray to me; I will carry it in."

I took it from her hand: she pointed me out the parlor door. The tray shook as I held it; the water spilt from the glass; my heart struck my ribs loud and fast. Mary opened the door for me, and shut it behind me.

This parlor looked gloomy: a neglected handful of fire burnt low in the grate; and, leaning over it, with his head supported against the high, old-fashioned mantelpiece, appeared the blind tenant of the room. His old dog, Pilot, lay on one side, removed out of the way, and coiled up as if afraid of being inadvertently trodden upon. Pilot pricked up his ears when I came in: then he jumped up with a yelp and a whine, and bounded towards me: he almost knocked the tray from my hands. I set it on the table; then patted him, and said softly, "Lie down!" Mr. Rochester turned mechanically to see what the commotion was: but as he saw nothing, he returned and sighed.

"Give me the water, Mary," he said.

I approached him with the now only half-filled glass; Pilot followed me, still excited.

"What is the matter?" he inquired.

"Down, Pilot!" I again said. He checked the water on its way to his lips, and seemed to listen: he drank, and put the glass down. "This is you, Mary, is it not?"

"Mary is in the kitchen," I answered.

He put out his hand with a quick gesture, but not seeing where I stood, he did not touch me. "Who is this? Who is this?" he demanded, trying, as it seemed, to see with those sightless eyes—unavailing and distressing attempt! "Answer me—speak again!" he ordered, imperiously and aloud.

"Will you have a little more water, sir? I spilt half of what was in the glass," I said.

"*Who* is it? *What* is it? Who speaks?"

"Pilot knows me, and John and Mary know I am here. I came only this evening," I answered.

"Great God!—what delusion has come over me? What sweet madness has seized me?"

"No delusion—no madness: your mind, sir, is too strong for delusion, your health too sound for frenzy."

"And where is the speaker? Is it only a voice? Oh! I *cannot* see, but I must feel, or my heart will stop and my brain burst. Whatever—whoever you are—be perceptible to the touch or I cannot live!"

He groped; I arrested his wandering hand, and prisoned it in both mine.

"Her very fingers!" he cried; "her small, slight fingers! If so there must be more of her."

The muscular hand broke from my custody; my arm was seized, my shoulder—neck—waist—I was entwined and gathered to him.

"Is it Jane? What is it? This is her shape—this is her size—"

"And this her voice," I added. "She is all here: her heart, too. God bless you, sir! I am glad to be so near you again."

"Jane Eyre!—Jane Eyre," was all he said.

"My dear master," I answered, "I am Jane Eyre: I have found you out—I am come back to you."

"In truth?—in the flesh? My living Jane?"

"You touch me, sir,—you hold me, and fast enough: I am not cold like a corpse, nor vacant like air, am I?"

"My living darling! These are certainly her limbs, and these her features; but I cannot be so blest, after all my misery. It is a dream; such dreams as I have had at night when I have clasped her once more to my heart, as I do now; and kissed her, as thus—and felt that she loved me, and trusted that she would not leave me."

"Which I never will, sir, from this day."

"Never will, says the vision? But I always woke and found it an empty mockery; and I was desolate and abandoned—my life dark, lonely, hopeless—my soul athirst and forbidden to drink—my heart famished and never to be fed. Gentle, soft dream, nestling in my arms now, you will fly, too, as your sisters have all fled before you: but kiss me before you go—embrace me, Jane."

"There, sir—and there!"'

I pressed my lips to his once brilliant and now rayless eyes—I swept his hair from his brow, and kissed that too. He suddenly seemed to arouse himself: the conviction of the reality of all this seized him.

"It is you—is it, Jane? You are come back to me then?"

"I am."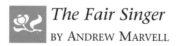

The Fair Singer

BY ANDREW MARVELL

To make a final conquest of all me,
Love did compose so sweet an enemy,
In whom both beauties to my death agree,
Joining themselves in fatal harmony;

That while she with her eyes my heart does
    bind,
She with her voice might captivate my mind.

I could have fled from one but singly fair:
My disentangled soul itself might save,
Breaking the curled trammels of her hair.
But how should I avoid to be her slave,
Whose subtle art invisibly can wreathe
My fetters of the very air I breathe?

It had been easy fighting in some plain,
Where victory might hang in equal choice,
But all resistance against her is vain,
Who has th' advantage both of eyes and voice,
And all my forces needs must be undone,
She having gained both the wind and sun. 🥀

A Glossary
of Dating Terms

Accidental sex: You didn't really mean to hook up, but you were both drunk and it just happened.

Al Gore: The guy who just won't accept that the relationship is over.

Bed arrest: The state of being stuck in bed cuddling with someone who won't let you get up. See also: Cuddle captive.

Beer goggles: Inebriated state in which someone you normally wouldn't find attractive suddenly starts to look pretty good.

Booty-call: A late-night phone call to someone you know who will come over for sex. Possible candidate: an ex you're on friendly terms with.

Buzzing the tower: Derived from the air force term for flying in low to check near the control tower, in dating terms "buzzing the tower" means doing a drive-by of your boyfriend/girlfriend's place, just checking to see if s/he's home.

Cuddle captive: The state of being stuck in bed post-sex with someone who won't let you get up. See also: Bed arrest.

Detour: A person you're dating until someone better comes along.

Hit on: Try to pick someone up, to make a move on someone. See also: Mack.

Mack: To overtly try to "score" with someone. See also: Hit on.

Mack Daddy: The suave guy who does a lot of macking.

Mailstrom: The obsessive watching of your email inbox and careful crafting of letters that occurs in the beginning of an email relationship.

Mr. (or Ms.) Right Now: A term for someone who isn't a keeper, but will fill the gap nicely until the real thing comes along.

Relationship karma: The bad things you did to your last significant other come back to haunt you with your next one.

Sexual camel: A person who can go long periods without sex.

SO: Significant other.

Three: The number of people you've slept with when your current lover asks, regardless of what the truth may be.

TMI (too much information): When someone

tells you more than you needed to know. For example, giving elaborate information on your bowel problems is probably not good first-date conversation.

Tonsil hockey: Making out in public to the point of obscenity.

Toxic bachelor: A guy who's handsome and romantic, but afraid to commit. He will date you for a short period of time, then run away.

Wuthering Heights
BY EMILY BRONTË

Catherine explains to her housekeeper why her love for Heathcliff must not ever be acknowledged, even as she rationalizes why she will marry Linton.

"I've no more business to marry Edgar Linton than I have to be in heaven; and if the wicked man in there had not brought Heathcliff so low, I shouldn't have thought of it. It would degrade me to marry Heathcliff now; so he shall never know how I love him: and that, not because he's handsome, Nelly, but because he's more myself than I am. Whatever our souls are made of, his and mine are the same; and Linton's is as different as a moonbeam from lightning, or frost from fire."

Sonnet #43, From the Portuguese
BY ELIZABETH BARRETT BROWNING

How do I love thee? Let me count the ways.
I love thee to the depth and breadth and height
My soul can reach, when feeling out of sight
For the ends of Being and ideal Grace.
I love thee to the level of everyday's
Most quiet need, by sun and candle-light.
I love thee freely, as men strive for Right;
I love thee purely, as they turn from Praise.
I love thee with the passion put to use
In my old griefs, and with my childhood's faith.
I love thee with a love I seemed to lose
With my lost saints!—I love thee with the
*   breath,*
Smiles, tears, of all my life!—and, if God choose,
I shall but love thee better after death.

CHAPTER III

Celebrating Love

*With you I will walk my path
from this day forward.*
—Wedding Vow

This chapter on celebrating your love with marriage and commitment ceremonies is just what it sounds like: a compendium of all things nuptial. Use it as a reference if you're looking for wedding ideas, or need to know what anniversary gift is appropriate for a particular year. Or just enjoy reading scenes of great weddings from literature; leaf through interviews with Las Vegas chapel employees.

If you're considering popping the question, you'll also find a variety of excellent proposal stories (including my own father's to my mother). And if you're having a non-traditional commitment ceremony, you'll find suggestions for vows and unusual folk customs from the world over that can be incorporated into your own special day.

The chapter is also peppered with quotes and aphorisms, suitable for a wedding toast or to be written in a card. You can also check out lists of great weddings from film and TV-land, and discover the most popular wedding songs used today. And hold on to your hat as you read some horror stories of the worst wedding nightmares ever (they just might inspire you to call off the ceremony and elope!).

If you are for pleasure, marry; if you prize rosy health, marry. A good wife is heaven's last best gift to man; his angel of mercy; minister of graces innumerable; his gem of many virtues; his casket of jewels.

—*T. L. Haines*

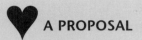 **A PROPOSAL**

The following letter appeared in the October 27, 2002, *New York Times Magazine's* Ethicist column (an advice column devoted to matters of practical ethical quandaries):

I have been dating a wonderful woman for the past year and a half, and your column has been a central part of our relationship. We eagerly await Sunday mornings, when we can lounge in bed or at brunch and debate your readers' weekly moral quandaries. We occasionally disagree with your responses, but we nearly always agree with each other's, which, I think, is a good sign. After all, you're only around once a week, and we don't have to share a bathroom with you. My question is this: "Will you marry me?" (And it's for Victoria, of course, not you.)

The Lion in Love
BY AESOP

A lion once fell in love with a beautiful maiden and proposed marriage to her parents. The people did not know what to say. They did not like to give their daughter to the Lion, yet they did not wish to enrage the King of Beasts. At last the father said: "We feel highly honored by your Majesty's proposal, but you see our daughter is a tender young thing, and we fear that in the vehemence of your affection you might possibly do her some injury. Might I venture to suggest that your Majesty should have your claws removed and your teeth extracted and we would gladly consider your proposal again." The Lion was so much in love that he had his claws trimmed and his big teeth taken out. But when he came again to the parents of the young girl they simply laughed in his face, and bade him do his worst.

Moral: Love can tame the wildest beast. 🌹

Take it from me, marriage isn't a word. . . it's a sentence!

—King Vidor

Sir Francis Bacon on Love

Born in 1561, Francis Bacon studied at Cambridge, and after his father's death left him penniless, he took up the study of law, and became a lawyer. His true passion was writing, however, and his many essays about his philosophies remain part of the canon of western literature. As you will see in the following excerpt from his essay on love, written in 1601, he doesn't think much of the sort of torrid passions that make men weak.

The stage is more beholding to love, that the life of man. For as to the stage, love is ever matter of comedies, and now and then of tragedies; but in life it doth much mischief; sometimes like a siren, sometimes like a fury.

You may observe that amongst all the great and worthy persons (whereof the memory remaineth, either ancient or recent) there is not one, that hath been transported to the mad degree of love: which shows that great spirits, and great business, do keep out this weak passion.

For there was never proud man thought so absurdly well of himself, as the lover doth of the person loved; and therefore it was well said that it is impossible to love, and to be wise. Neither doth this weakness appear to others only, and not to the party loved; but to the loved most of all, except the love be reciproque. For it is a true rule, that love is ever rewarded, either with the reciproque, or with an inward and secret contempt. By how much the more, men ought to beware of this passion, which loseth not only other things, but itself!

They do best, who if they cannot but admit love, yet make it keep quarters; and sever it wholly from their serious affairs, and actions, of life; for if it check once with business, it troubleth men's fortunes, and maketh men, that they can no ways be true to their own ends. I know not how, but martial men are given to love: I think, it is but as they are given to wine; for perils commonly ask to be paid in pleasures. There is in man's nature, a secret inclination and motion, towards love of others, which if it be not spent upon some one or a few, doth naturally spread itself towards many, and maketh men become humane and charitable; as it is seen sometime in friars. Nuptial love maketh mankind; friendly love perfecteth it; but wanton love corrupteth, and embaseth it.

On Taking a Wife
BY THOMAS MOORE

"Come, come," said Tom's father, "At your
   time of life,
There's no longer excuse for thus playing
   the rake.
It's time you should think, boy, of taking
   a wife."
"Why, so it is, Father. Whose wife shall
   I take?"

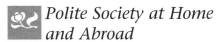

Polite Society at Home and Abroad

BY ANNIE RANDALL WHITE, ©1901

This turn-of-the-century etiquette book lists all the formal dos and don'ts for weddings of the day. While much of the advice seems dated, it is interesting to note how much the formal wedding ceremonies of today stay true to the traditional ceremonies described in this book.

CHOOSING BRIDES-MAIDS

The brides-maids should be a little younger than the bride. These should be from two to six in number, and they should exercise taste in dress, looking as pretty as possible, being careful, however, not to outshine the bride. White is the accepted dress for brides-maids, but they are not limited to this. They can select light and delicate colours, showing care that everything harmonises. Pink, blue, sea-green, ecru, or lavender, makes a very pretty contrast to the bride, who should invariably be clothed in white.

The addition of some pretty children under ten, who follow the brides-maids in the procession to the altar, and who are called flower-girls, is a beautiful innovation.

THE WEDDING-RING CEREMONY

The wedding-ring is used in the marriage service of nearly all denominations. It is always a plain gold band, no longer heavy and solid, but a rather narrow circlet. The use of the wedding-ring is a very ancient custom. It is probable that it was used by the Swiss Lake dwellers, and other primitive people. In very early times it was common among the Hebrews, who possibly borrowed it from the Egyptians, among whom, as well as the Greeks and Romans, the wedding-ring was worn.

An English book on etiquette, published in 1732, says, the bride may choose on which finger the ring shall be placed, and it says some brides prefer the thumb, others the index finger, others the middle finger, "because it is the largest," and others the fourth finger, because "a vein proceeds from it to the heart."

The engagement ring is removed at the altar by the bridegroom, who passes the wedding-ring (a plain gold band, with the date and the initials engraved inside) to the clergyman, to be used by him in the ceremony. On the way home from church, or as soon thereafter as convenient, the bridegroom may put the engagement ring back on the bride's finger, to stand over its precious fellow.

Some husbands who like to observe these pretty little fancies, present their wives of a year's standing with another ring, either chased or plain, to be worn on the wedding-ring finger, and which is called the "keeper." This, too, is supposed to "stand guard" over the wedding ring.

DRESS OF THE BRIDE

The dress of the bride should be devised according to her means or taste. A veil may or may not be worn; one composed of tulle is more dainty in its effect than a lace one. But for a very fleshy bride lace will be best, as tulle has the quality of making one's proportions look larger. The orange blossom has always been adopted for ornamentation, and is very beautiful. But if these cannot be procured, other natural flowers can take their place. If jewelry is worn, it should be something very elegant and chaste.

AVOID SHOW OF AFFECTION

If a tour is made, avoid any silly manifestations of affection in public. Observe a respectful reserve toward each other; thus you will not expose yourself to ridicule by demonstrations of affection which should be kept for the sacred privacy of home.

A HINT TO THE FUTURE HUSBAND

Don't haunt the house of your loved one for a few days previous to the wedding. There are many matters to be attended to, requiring her counseling with her elders, and long interviews tire and annoy her. Besides, a loving daughter naturally desires to be with her mother for the few days left her. She is none the less loyal to you for this affection for her mother, and you will be none the loser for your forbearance. 🌹

There was an old party of Lyme
Who married three wives at
  a time
When asked, "Why the third?"
He replied, "One's absurd,
And bigamy, sir, is a crime."

—Anonymous

A PROPOSAL

He was a young lawyer, living in Pittsburgh. His girlfriend, also a lawyer, was living in New Jersey. The long-distance relationship wasn't ideal, but they had been dating since graduate school, and they hoped to find jobs in the same city. He called her to cancel one of their planned weekends together, citing a regrettable last-minute case that required him to work through the weekend.

(continued)

Disheartened, she stayed in and went to bed early, even putting on the proverbial ugly face mask as she puttered around her apartment, sad that her boyfriend wouldn't be making it there for the weekend. During the evening, he called her several times, just to chat. In fact, he was calling her from the road, and he kept calling back so that she wouldn't call him and discover he wasn't home.

His final call came so late he woke her up. "Look outside your window," he said. He was outside, sitting on his car, holding a bottle of champagne and two glasses. When she went outside, surprised to see him, he asked her to marry him.

Where there's marriage without love, there will be love without marriage.

—*Benjamin Franklin*

 *Emma*
BY JANE AUSTEN

In Jane Austen's *Emma*, the title character modestly discusses the role she played in the marriage of her friend Miss Taylor to a local widower. Matchmaking is an art, she says, and one at which she excels. Of course, Jane Austen's dry wit makes it clear that there is some question as to whether Emma really did very much at all to make the marriage happen.

"And you have forgotten one matter of joy to me," said Emma, "and a very considerable one—that I made the match myself. I made the match, you know, four years ago; and to have it take place, and be proved in the right, when so many people said Mr. Weston would never marry again, may comfort me for any thing."

Mr. Knightley shook his head at her. Her father fondly replied, "Ah! my dear, I wish you would not make matches and foretell things, for whatever you say always comes to pass. Pray do not make any more matches."

"I promise you to make none for myself, papa; but I must, indeed, for other people. It is the greatest amusement in the world! And after such success, you know!—Every body said that Mr. Weston would never marry again. Oh dear, no! Mr. Weston, who had been a widower so long, and who seemed so perfectly comfortable without a wife, so constantly occupied either in his business in town or among his friends here, always acceptable wherever he went, always cheerful—Mr. Weston need not spend a single evening in the year alone if he did not like it. Oh no! Mr. Weston certainly would never marry again. Some people even talked of a promise to his wife on her deathbed, and others of the son and the uncle not letting him. All manner of solemn nonsense was talked on the subject, but I believed none of it.

"Ever since the day—about four years ago—that Miss Taylor and I met with him in Broadway Lane, when, because it began to drizzle, he darted away with so much gallantry, and borrowed two umbrellas for us from Farmer Mitchell's, I made up my mind on the subject. I planned the match from that hour; and when such success has blessed me in this instance, dear papa, you cannot think that I shall leave off match-making."

"I do not understand what you mean by 'success,'" said Mr. Knightley. "Success supposes endeavour. Your time has been properly and delicately spent, if you have been endeavouring for the last four years to bring about this marriage. A worthy employment for a young lady's mind! But if, which I rather imagine, your making the match, as you call it, means only your planning it, your saying to yourself one idle day, 'I think it would be a very good thing for Miss Taylor if Mr. Weston were to marry her,' and saying it again to yourself every now and then afterwards, why do you talk of success? Where is your merit? What are you proud of? You made a lucky guess; and that is all that can be said."

"And have you never known the pleasure and triumph of a lucky guess?—I pity you.—I thought you cleverer—for, depend upon it a lucky guess is never merely luck. There is always some talent in it. And as to my poor word 'success,' which you quarrel with, I do not know that I am so entirely without any claim to it. You have drawn two pretty pictures; but I think there may be a third—a something between the do-nothing and the do-all. If I had not promoted Mr. Weston's visits here, and given many little encouragements, and smoothed many little matters, it might not have come to anything after all."

A PROPOSAL

The man had a ceramic plate made up with the words, "Will You Marry Me" on it. He took his girlfriend to dinner at a local steakhouse. The guy had arranged it with the management that his girlfriend's dinner would be served on that plate.

Of course, she couldn't see the writing on the plate when her dinner was served, but as she was completing her meal, she saw the proposal message on her plate. As she became aware of what had been there all along, the guy got down on one knee beside her with a ring.

A good marriage would be between a blind wife and a deaf husband.

—Michel de Montaigne

The Modern Marriage Market

The following excerpts are a serialized book that appeared in an English women's magazine, *The Lady's Realm,* in 1897, and were later published as a series of essays all about the state of marriage in such "modern" times.

What is marriage? Many of you have, I think, forgotten. It is not the church, the ritual, the blessing of the clergyman, or the ratifying and approving presence of one's friends and relations at the ceremony,—still less is it a matter of "settlements" and expensive millinery. It is the taking of a solemn vow before the Throne of the Eternal,—a vow which declares that the man and woman concerned have discovered in each other his and her true mate,—that they feel life is alone valuable and worth living in each other's company,—that they are prepared to endure trouble, poverty, pain, sickness, death itself, provided they may only be together,—and that all the world is a mere grain of dust in worth as compared to the exalted passion which fills their souls and moves them to become one in flesh as well as one in spirit. Nothing can make marriage an absolutely sacred thing except the great love, combined with the pure and faithful intention, of the human pair involved.

—Marie Corelli

After an early stage of existence, men are much less likely to "fall in love," as it is called, than women, and especially girls who are less in contact with the real world, and unacquainted with its sterner side. It is therefore far more important that they should be protected against themselves, and it is certainly the plain duty of every mother to lay before her child the inevitable consequences of an imprudent marriage.

Most girls in the upper classes know nothing of the value of money; they are brought up in comfortable, or even luxurious, homes, by parents generally indulgent, and are as incapable of judging of the merits of a possible husband as they would be of the points of a horse. Such a girl might, as likely as not, choose a high-stepping, flashy screw, and pay for it the ruinous price of a spoilt life. It is the act of a friend, though a painful task, to tear aside the veil which ignorance or native innocence and a pure heart hang before her eyes, if by so doing she can be saved from an irretrievable blunder, the punishment for which is as heavy, alas! as for a crime.

Girls are now highly educated—so far as book-learning can make them so; they are allowed freedom undreamt of twenty years ago, and the superficial knowledge of life they thus acquire is one of the most dangerous elements in their present condition. An attitude of independence, an indisposition to listen to advice, combined with total ignorance of the real situation they are bent on creating for themselves, is a spectacle which would be ludicrous if it were not melancholy to those who know by experience the difficulties which beset a woman's life, even under the most favoured conditions.

It is therefore inevitable that marriage should produce a large amount of disappointment, which may best be overcome by reflecting on our own shortcomings rather than on those of our companion. Partners in a happy marriage must bring a certain capital of youth and health, and in addition qualities, moral and mental, such as are necessary to advance them in their condition of life.

"Choose not alone a proper mate,
But a proper time to marry."

—Susan,
Countess of Malmesbury

Love is the triumph of imagination over intelligence.

—*H. L. Mencken*

Marriage is the triumph of imagination over intelligence. Second marriage is the triumph of hope over experience.

—*Oscar Wilde*

A PROPOSAL

He and I had determined that I would have Proposal and Ring just after his parents and extended family met me at the Thanksgiving Day gala feast at his parents' home in Jackson Heights, it being more seemly to conservative Viennese parents to give their input. That was the plan. One night in mid-November, your father said tenderly to me, "Sweetheart, if you really promise not to tell absolutely anyone about it, I'll ask you to marry me right now." P.S. He had the ring at the ready and did not understand why I did not think it was a very romantic proposal. Later, after I knew him better, I did.

ADVICE TO A MAN WHO WISHES TO MARRY

This advice, excerpted from *The Royal Path of Life: Aims and Aids to Success and Happiness* by T.L. Haines, A.M. and L.W. Yaggy, M.S., ©1882, still resonates today, as the authors warn young men to avoid women who are selfish or fickle. And above all, avoid the siren's smile!

If you intend to marry, if you think your happiness will be increased and your interest advanced by matrimony, be sure and "look where you're going." Join yourself in union with no woman who is selfish, for she will sacrifice you; with no one who is fickle, for she will become estranged; have naught to do with a proud one for she will ruin you. Leave a coquette to the fools who flutter around her; let her own fireside accommodate a scold; and flee from a woman who loves scandal as you would flee from the evil one.

"Look where you are going" will sum it all up. Gaze not on beauty too much, lest it blast thee; nor too long, lest it blind thee; nor too near, lest it burn thee: if thou like it, it deceives thee; if thou love it, it disturbs thee; if thou lust after it, it destroys thee; if virtue accompany it, it is the heart's paradise; if vice associate it, it is the soul's purgatory; it is the wise man's bonfire, and the fool's furnace. The Godless youth is infatuated by a fair face, and is lured to his fate by a siren's smile.

WHY A MAN NEEDS A WIFE

A judicious wife is always snipping off from her husband's moral nature little twigs that are growing in the wrong direction. She keeps him in shape by continual pruning. If you say anything silly, she will affectionately tell you so. If you declare you will do some absurd thing, she will find the means of preventing you from doing it.

The wisest things which a man commonly does are those which his wife counsels him to do. A wife is the grand wielder of the moral pruning knife. When you see a man appearing shabby, hair uncombed, and no buttons on his coat, nine times out of ten you are correct in concluding that he is a bachelor. You can conclude much of the same when you see a man profane, or speaking vulgarly of ladies. We would add that young men who wish to appear well in every respect should get married. It has been well said, "A man unmarried is but half a man."

A sound marriage is not based on complete frankness; it is based on a sensible reticence.

—*Morris L. Ernst*

A PROPOSAL

In the New York media world, everybody who's anybody reads the Starr Report, a column about showbiz happenings, in *The New York Post*. So it was a pretty sure bet for one enterprising suitor that his would-be bride would be reading the column on the morning of October 18, 2002. And so it was that Tracey Spector, along with half of New York, read this in her copy of the morning:

"This just in. . .

I have a personal message for Fox News Channel publicist Tracey Spector: If you're reading this right now, go to the empty office next door. Bryan is waiting there with flowers—and he has something he wants to ask you."

Her answer was duly reported a few days later. Seems the whole story sparked quite a bit of interest among *Post* readers! From the Sunday, October 20th *New York Post*: "This just in. . .

To everyone that called and emailed: Yes, Fox News Channel publicist Tracey Spector did, indeed, agree to marry Bryan Reyhani after reading about Bryan's intentions in Friday's Starr Report. Tracey screamed, ran into the office next to hers, and happily accepted Bryan's proposal. Good luck to them both!"

(continued)

The Background: Building a Proposal

Behind the scenes, Bryan had been planning this for several weeks. He spoke with Tracey's boss and several of her coworkers, who helped arrange the place (an unused office next to Tracey's) and made sure she had her copy of *The New York Post* on the big day.

Tracey explains, "As part of my job, I read all the daily papers, but the *Post* isn't usually delivered with the rest of the papers, so I have to pick it up myself on the way into work." On that day, she notes, her coworker made sure to leave a copy of the paper right on top of the usual stack, and since Tracey had picked up a copy herself, she had two copies of the same paper. That's funny, she thought, as she noticed the duplicate, but as long as its here, I might as well read the *Post* first today.

Meanwhile, Bryan had a bunch of flowers and had settled into the office next door over an hour beforehand. Tracey recalls, "I was late to work that day, about a half-hour after my usual time," As she sorted through her email, she wondered why there wasn't a message from Bryan that day, since he usually sent one every morning. In fact, she says, she emailed a friend of hers to discuss the lack of Bryan's customary morning greeting. "What do you think it means?" she wrote.

But before too long, she got to the Starr Report column and all was clear. Thrilled and genuinely surprised, she ran into the office next door, where Bryan had been waiting for over an hour. "Yes!" she told him happily, and they both knew this would be a romantic proposal story they would be telling for years to come.

Leap Year Proposals

In the formal days of yore, it would have been unheard of for a woman to issue a proposal to a man (or for a same-sex couple to have a proposal, for that matter!), but there was always one special allowance. Leap Year Day (February 29, which comes but once every four years) was traditionally marked by a topsy-turvy state of affairs in which a woman had the power to ask for a man's hand. Furthermore, the rule was this: Not only may a woman ask a man to marry her, he must by law say yes!

Legend has it that this Leap Year rule dates back to 1288, when Queen Margaret of Scotland allegedly decreed that on February 29—a day that had no legal status in English law—a woman could propose to any man of her choosing, and unless he was already betrothed to another, he was required by order of the Queen's royal decree to say yes.

Unfortunately, although this so-called Scottish Law has been cited all over the globe, it turns out to be an urban myth; for no such decree was ever made. Still, there is something compelling about keeping the tradition of Leap Year—and not just the day but the entire year— as a time when women are encouraged to be especially empowered!

Marriage is a wonderful invention; but, then again, so is a bicycle repair kit.

—Billy Connolly

The Best Man

The custom of having a best man originated around A.D. 200 with the German Goths. Because sometimes the bride had been forcefully carried off to the wedding, it became a tradition that the groom be flanked by his "right-hand man" to help ensure that the bride wasn't "stolen back" by her vengeful relations. The job of the best man, therefore, was literally to fight off any problems that might develop during the ceremony. In time, the position came to have a more benign role in the wedding, that of the groom's best friend, the holder of the ring.

Marriage is popular because it combines the maximum of temptation with the maximum of opportunity.

—George Bernard Shaw

A RING OF LOVE

Some historians believe that the custom of exchanging rings goes back as far as Egypt's third dynasty where circles symbolized eternity and the circle of life. Later, the Romans made the rings out of gold. The Greeks in the third century B.C. believed that the ring-finger has the "vein amoris," the vein of love, which runs straight to the heart; therefore, the ring was placed on the third finger.

During medieval times, it was said that the ring was placed on the hand closest to the heart. By counting the fingers as the Father, the Son, and the Holy Ghost, the ring was placed on the third finger. Interestingly, not all cultures wear rings on the so-called "ring finger."

Early Hebrew women used to wear the ring on the middle finger, and in India some woman wear the rings on their thumbs.

I think men who have a pierced ear are better prepared for marriage. They've experienced pain and bought jewelry.

—Rita Rudner

WEDDING VOWS

A wedding can be as traditional or unusual as the couple wishes to make it. Collected here are some of the most common vows, as well as suggestions of vows for use in non-traditional weddings and/or commitment ceremonies.

 The Book of Common Prayer

The standard wedding vows from *The Book of Common Prayer* are what most people think of when they hear the phrase "wedding vows." The book was written in 1559, and the following vows may be the oldest words so familiar to modern ears.

Minister: (to groom) Wilt thou have this Woman to be thy wedded wife, to live together after God's ordinance in the holy estate of Matrimony? Wilt thou love her, comfort her, honor, and keep her in sickness and in health; and, forsaking all others, keep thee only unto her, so long as ye both shall live?

Man: I will.

Minister: (to bride) Wilt thou have this Man to thy wedded husband, to live together after God's ordinance in the holy estate of Matrimony? Wilt thou love him, comfort him, honor, and keep him in sickness and in health; and, forsaking all others, keep thee only unto him, so long as ye both shall live?

Woman: I will.

STANDARD CIVIL CEREMONY

The words may differ slightly from state to state, but the general gist is the same. These simple vows are used by both parties, and get to the point simply and graciously.

(Name), I take you to be my lawfully wedded (husband/wife).

Before these witnesses I vow to love you and care for you as long as we both shall live.

I take you, with all your faults and your strengths, as I offer myself to you with my faults and my strengths.

I will help you when you need help, and will turn to you when I need help.

I choose you as the person with whom I will spend my life.

NON-TRADITIONAL VOWS

These can be edited to suit any couple. They are suitable not just for weddings, but for any public commitment ceremony.

Today, (name), I join my life to yours, not merely as your (partner), but as your friend, your lover, and your confidant.

Let me be the shoulder you lean on, the rock on which you rest, the companion of your life.

With you I will walk my path from this day forward.

On this day, (month, day, year), I, (name), join myself to you (name), before this company.

May our days be long, and may they be seasoned with love, understanding and respect.

Before these witnesses I, (name), vow to love you, (name), and care for you as long as we both shall live.

I take you, with all your faults and your strengths, as I offer myself to you with my faults and my strengths.

I will help you when you need help, and will turn to you when I need help.

I choose you as the person with whom I will spend my life.

Someone once asked me why women don't gamble as much as men do and I gave the commonsensical reply that we don't have as much money. That was a true but incomplete answer. In fact, women's total instinct for gambling is satisfied by marriage.

—Gloria Steinem

Blind, Mathilde: The Heather on Fire, a Tale of Highland Clearances
BY SIR WALTER SCOTT

I.

ROSE now the longed-for, long-delaying hour
To which, as towards the sun the sunwar
    flower,
Their hearts had turned though many a year
    of life,
When Michael should take Mary unto wife.
Long, long before the laggard sun arose
Flushing the hill-sides' freshly fallen snows,
The bride and bridegroom, in their best array,
Footed it to the kirk on this their wedding day.

II.

At home the neighbours, full of kindly zest,
Prepared the feast for many a wedding guest;
Swept out the barns and scoured the dusky byres;
Piled high the peats and kindled roaring fires,
Whose merry flames in golden eddies broke
Round ancient cauldrons crusted o'er with smoke,
Whence an inviting savour steaming rose,
As, slowly bubbling, boiled the meaty barley
    brose.

III.

Spread was the board; the various kinds
    of meat,
Or roast or stew, sent up a savour sweet,
Grateful to Highlanders, whose frugal cheer
Is broth and oatmeal porridge all the year.

But on this happy day no stint there was
For all who liked to come and take their glass
Of the good whisky, and with heart zest
Drink to the new-wed pair with many a
    boisterous jest.

IV.

From township, bothie, shieling, miles away,
The guests had flocked to grace this festive day:
The shepherd left his fold, the lass her byre,
Old folks their ingle-nook beside the fire,
Mothers their bairns—yea, half the country-side
Turned out to hail the strapping groom and bride;
And jolly pipers scaled the break-neck passes,
With frolic tunes to rouse the lightsome lads
    and lasses.

• • •

XX.

*And as they fling, and cling, and wheel, and
    pass,*
Many a lover lightly hugs his lass;
And many a village belle and queen of hearts
Makes desperate havoc with her simple arts
*'Mid her adoring swains, who, while they
    shower*
Their melting glances on her, glare and glower
Upon their rivals, whom, while meekly sighing,
*With many a fervid kick they fain would send
    a-flying.*

XXI.

But still among the bonnie dancers there
Michael and Mary were the bonniest pair:
So tall and stately, moving 'mid the rout
*Of flushed and panting couples, wrapped
    about*

With the pure glory of love, which seemed
   to fill
And permeate their features with a still
And tender glow—impassioned yet serene,
The scripture of true hearts revealed in rustic
   mien.

XXII.

On, on they whirled to many a loud strathspey,
Long after groom and bride had gone away;
Long after the late half-moon's dwindling
   light
Had risen grisly on the snowy night,
Through which the wind, in sudden fits and
   spasms,
Went roaring through the roaring mountain
   chasms,
And then fell silent—with a piercing cry,
Like a sore-hunted beast in its last agony!

XXIII.

But oh, what cared these merry wedding-guests,
With flying pulses and with throbbing breasts,
For all the piping winds and palely snows!—
Their pipes out-played the wind-notes, and
   their toes
Out-whirled the whirling snowflakes, and
   bright eyes
Did very well instead of starry skies;
And as the winter night grew drear and drearier,
Music and mountain dew but made them all
   the cheerier.

XXIV.

And so the wedding lasted full three days,
With dance and song kept at a roaring pace,
And drinking no whit slacker; then the feast
Came to an end at last, and many a beast—
Rough Highland sheltie, or sure-footed ass—

Carried them safe o'er stream and mountain
*   pass,*
Through treacherous mosses and by darkling
*   wood,*
Till safe and sound once more by their own
*   hearths they stood.* ❧

WEDDING TRADITIONS

There are many traditions, some old, some fairly new, that couples may enjoy adding to their weddings or commitment ceremonies. Most of these are not specific to any religion, or even to a formal wedding, but rather can be used by any people wishing to personalize their public declarations of love.

THE ROSE CEREMONY

In the Rose Ceremony, the intended couple gives each other a red rose. Two roses are all that is necessary to perform it. The exchange is generally placed at the end of the ceremony, just before the official pronouncement that the couple is now joined.

In the language of flowers, a single red rose symbolizes true love, and this simple ceremony is a very public yet personal declaration of the love between the participants, without any words needing to be spoken.

THE UNITY CEREMONY

In this ceremony, each member of the couple holds a lighted candle, which they then use together to light a third candle, symbolizing their union. The officiant will then say something along these lines:

"(Name) and (name), the two separate candles symbolize your separate lives, separate families and separate sets of friends. I ask that each of you take one of the lit candles and that together you light the center candle.

The individual candles represent your lives before today. Lighting the center candle represents that your two lives are now joined to one light, and represents the joining together of your two families and sets of friends to one."

ORANGE BLOSSOMS

The wearing of orange blossoms by the bride is an old custom. In ancient China, orange blossoms were emblems of purity, chastity, and innocence, which is why they were often used as part of a bride's costume.

The orange tree has long been a symbol of fruitfulness; it is one of the rare plants that simultaneously blooms and bears fruit. During the time of the Crusades, the orange-blossom custom was brought from the Far East to Western Europe, by way of Spain, then France, then England. By the early 1800s, many enchanting legends had spread throughout the continent of maidens entwining fresh orange blossoms into a bridal wreath for their hair. The idea that orange blossoms were a wedding flower became so central to western culture that the phrase "to gather orange blossoms" came to mean "to seek a wife."

THE CHEROKEE PRAYER

"God in heaven above, please protect the ones we love. We honor all you created as we pledge our hearts and lives together. We honor Mother Earth, and ask for our marriage to be abundant and grow stronger through the seasons; we honor fire, and ask that our union be warm and glowing with love in our hearts; we honor wind, and ask that we sail though life safe and calm as in our father's arms; we honor water, to clean and soothe our relationship, that it may never thirst for love. With all the forces of the universe you created, we pray for harmony and true happiness as we forever grow young together. Amen."

IRISH WEDDING TRADITIONS

When choosing a wedding date, avoid the month of May! As the superstition has it, "Marry in May and rue the day." Other Irish wedding traditions include:

The lucky horseshoe: The horseshoe has long been a symbol of good luck, and Irish brides used to carry real ones on their wedding day! However, if you'd prefer something smaller, you can find porcelain horseshoes to tuck into the dress, or fabric horseshoes that can be worn around the wrist.

Little bells: The chiming of bells is supposed to keep evil spirits away, restore harmony if a couple is fighting, and also remind a couple of their wedding. You may want to hand out tiny bells to your guests to ring after the ceremony, or at the reception in lieu of clinking glasses to request that the bride and groom kiss.

BREAKING THE GLASS

There is a Jewish custom of placing a wine-glass, usually wrapped in a cloth napkin, near the groom's right foot, and the groom shatters it to conclude the marriage ceremony. The congregation usually responds with "mazel tov" so that the couple should be blessed with good luck. There are several common reasons given for the 800-year-old tradition: Some say the glass is broken to recall the destruction of Jerusalem and the Holy Temple. Others believe the shattered glass reminds us of how fragile life is, and it is broken as a reminder that the marriage should stay intact despite life's fragility. Still others say that since a shattered glass can never be whole again, the breaking of the glass is a symbol of the great important change that has taken place, since a marriage is a life-changing event that cannot be altered.

AFRICAN WEDDING TRADITIONS

In the Sudan, dancers toss wedding flowers all over the bride and groom to ensure a fragrant future for the new couple. A mixture of turmeric rice, coins, and candy is thrown at the couple as they leave the ceremony. Rice is a symbol of prosperity, and the turmeric gives it a yellow color, for everlasting love. The coins remind the couple to share their wealth with the less fortunate, and the candy bestows sweetness upon their marriage.

In South Africa, twelve important symbols of life are often incorporated into the wedding ceremony: wine, wheat, pepper, salt, bitter herbs, water, a pot and spoon, a broom, honey, a spear, a shield, and a copy of the Bible or Koran.

BIBLE VERSES

There are many Bible verses suitable for inclusion in a wedding ceremony, but here are two of the most commonly used:

Matthew 19:5–6
And said, For this cause shall a man leave father and mother, and shall cleave to his wife: and they twain shall be one flesh?

Wherefore they are no more twain, but one flesh. What therefore God hath joined together, let not man put asunder.

Proverbs 18:22
Whoso findeth a wife findeth a good thing, and obtaineth favor of the Lord.

SO YOU WANT TO OFFICIATE AT A WEDDING

The Universal Life Church is a non-denominational church that ordains anyone a legal minister, free of charge. As a Universal Life Church minister, you will be legally allowed to officiate at weddings. You can also perform baptisms, funerals, and more. The ULC promotes freedom of religion, and they do not require any particular beliefs or religious affiliations in their ministers. To find out more about getting your free certification in the church, you can visit their website at www.ulc.org/hq, or contact them at 2159 S. Sky Tanner Drive, Tucson, AZ, 85748; 520-721-2882.

Little Women
BY LOUISA MAY ALCOTT

Meg looked very like a rose herself, for all that was best and sweetest in heart and soul seemed to bloom into her face that day, making it fair and tender, with a charm more beautiful than beauty. Neither silk, lace, nor orange flowers would she have. "I don't want a fashionable wedding, but only those about me whom I love, and to them I wish to look and be my familiar self."

So she made her wedding gown herself, sewing into it the tender hopes and innocent romances of a girlish heart. Her sisters braided up her pretty hair, and the only ornaments she wore were the lilies of the valley, which "her John" liked best of all the flowers that grew.

"You do look just like our own dear Meg, only so very sweet and lovely that I should hug you if it wouldn't crumple your dress," cried Amy, surveying her with delight when all was done.

"Then I am satisfied. But please hug and kiss me, everyone, and don't mind my dress. I want a great many crumples of this sort put into it today." And Meg opened her arms to her sisters, who clung about her with April faces for a minute, feeling that the new love had not changed the old.

"Now I'm going to tie John's cravat for him, and then to stay a few minutes with Father quietly in the study." And Meg ran down to perform these little ceremonies, and then to follow her mother wherever she went, conscious that in spite of the smiles on the motherly face, there was a secret sorrow hid in the motherly heart at the flight of the first bird from the nest.

As the younger girls stand together, giving the last touches to their simple toilet, it may be a good time to tell of a few changes which three years have wrought in their appearance, for all are looking their best just now. . . . All three wore suits of thin silver gray (their best gowns for the summer), with blush roses in hair and bosom, and all three looked just what they were, fresh-faced, happy-hearted girls, pausing a moment in their busy lives to read with wistful eyes the sweetest chapter in the romance of womanhood.

There were to be no ceremonious performances, everything was to be as natural and homelike as possible, so when Aunt March arrived, she was scandalized to see the bride come running to welcome and lead her in, to find the bridegroom fastening up a garland that had fallen down, and to catch a glimpse of the paternal minister marching upstairs with a grave countenance and a wine bottle under each arm.

"Upon my word, here's a state of things!" cried the old lady, taking the seat of honor prepared for her, and settling the folds of her lavender moire with a great rustle. "You oughtn't to be seen till the last minute, child."

"I'm not a show, Aunty, and no one is coming to stare at me, to criticize my dress, or count the cost of my luncheon. I'm too happy to care what anyone says or thinks, and I'm going to have my little wedding just as I like it. John, dear, here's your hammer." And away went Meg to help "that man" in his highly improper employment. . . .

There was no bridal procession, but a sudden silence fell upon the room as Mr. March and the young couple took their places under the green arch. Mother and sisters gathered close, as if loath to give Meg up. The fatherly voice broke more than once, which only seemed to make the service more beautiful and solemn. The bride-groom's hand trembled visibly, and no one heard his replies. But Meg looked straight up in her husband's eyes, and said, "I will!" with such tender trust in her own face and voice that her mother's heart rejoiced and Aunt March sniffed audibly. ❧

Wedding Nightmares

"Well, the day of their wedding . . . the groom was waiting patiently for his bride, and so were all the guests, 45 minutes past the time the wedding was supposed to start, when finally the bride showed up. She scurried down the aisle after her two bridesmaids, and the pastor said his part, then began to ask them to repeat after him. When it got to the bride's turn, she slurred her words, skipping words, and actually said some pretty bizarre stuff. The chick was toasted! Drunk as a skunk! Three sheets to the wind! And on her wedding day!"

"I go ahead and walk down the aisle, and halfway down, a guest stands up, and announces he was supposed to get the ice for the reception and he forgot—could we wait while he took care of that? I looked him dead in the eye and said, 'You are kidding, right?' His response was, 'It'll only take me fifteen minutes.' Nobody said a word—we just all stared at him. Finally I told him to sit down and wait until the ceremony was over. He sat down, but he gave me the *dirtiest* look!"

"I'm a computer tech. One guest brought a computer to my wedding, hoping I would fix it. I'd never dreamed I'd be so happy to have my wedding *over with*."

"Then it really got good. They were over by the cake and the cake knife, which really wasn't a cake knife, but some sort of sword the groom had picked up in his military travels and thought would be great to cut the cake with. Everyone could tell that the bride was growing angrier and angrier. Nobody was eating. Everyone was watching them. The groom grabs her arm. Remember the cake sword. She swung it at him! Apparently, he had learned how to move fast in the Navy. One of the groomsmen got between them, but he did get cut, though thankfully, not seriously—but on a white uniform it looked like the guy was bleeding to death. . . . The marriage was annulled."

Go to www.etiquettehell.com/wedindex.htm to read the full stories.

Most Popular Wedding Songs

According to a national survey, these are the most popular wedding songs:

Pachelbel's *Canon in D*

"Butterfly Kisses," Bob Carlisle

"At Last," Etta Jones

"Amazed," Lonestar

"From This Moment," Shania Twain

"It's Your Love," Tim McGraw

"Hero," Enrique Iglesias

"The Wedding March (Here Comes the Bride)"from Wagner's *Lohengrin*

"Daddy's Little Girl," Kippi Brannon

Keep your eyes wide open before marriage, half shut afterwards.

—Benjamin Franklin

 *Anna Karenina*

BY COUNT LEO TOLSTOY

When the ceremony of plighting troth was over, the beadle spread before the lectern in the middle of the church a piece of pink silken stuff, the choir sang a complicated and elaborate psalm, in which the bass and tenor sang responses to one another, and the priest turning round pointed the bridal pair to the pink silk rug. . . . After the customary questions, whether they desired to enter upon matrimony, and whether they were pledged to anyone else, and their answers, which sounded strange to themselves, a new ceremony began. Kitty listened to the words of the prayer, trying to make out their meaning, but she could not. The feeling of triumph and radiant happiness flooded her soul more and more as the ceremony went on, and deprived her of all power of attention. . . . "That's all splendid," thought Kitty, catching the words, "all that's just as it should be," and a smile of happiness, unconsciously reflected in everyone who looked at her, beamed on her radiant face.

"Put it on quite," voices were heard urging when the priest had put on the wedding crowns and Shtcherbatsky, his hand shaking in its three-button glove, held the crown high above her head. "Put it on!" she whispered, smiling. Levin looked round at her, and was struck by the joyful radiance on her face, and unconsciously her feeling infected him. He too, like her felt glad and happy. They enjoyed hearing the epistle read, and the roll of the head deacon's voice at the last verse, awaited with such impatience by the outside public. They enjoyed drinking out of the shallow cup of warm red wine and water, and they were still more pleased when the priest, flinging back his stole and taking both their hands in his, led them round the lectern to the accompaniment of bass voices chanting "Glory to God." . . . The spark of joy kindled in Kitty seemed to have infected everyone in the church. It seemed to Levin that the priest and the deacon too wanted to smile just as he did.

Taking the crowns off their heads the priest read the last prayer and congratulated the young people. Levin looked at Kitty, and he had never before seen her look as she did. She was charming with the new radiance of happiness in her face. Levin longed to say something to her, but he did not know whether it was all over. The priest got him out of his difficulty. He smiled his kindly smile and said gently, "Kiss your wife, and you kiss your husband," and took the candles out of their hands. Levin kissed her smiling lips with timid care, gave her his arm, and with a new strange sense of closeness, walked out of the church. He did not believe, he could not believe, that it was true. It was only when their wondering and timid eyes met that he believed in it, because he felt that they were one. 🌿

VIVA LAS VEGAS!

There are over 100 wedding chapels in downtown Las Vegas, and they offer packages ranging from a simple civil ceremony to a drive-through Elvis extravaganza. Want to get married in a hot-air balloon? Have a hankering for one or more celebrity impersonators at your wedding? Then Las Vegas is the place for you!

"We've had people show up in boats, on horses and bikes, in limos and cabs, even on their way to work," says a source who works at the Little White Chapel in Vegas. Indeed, you could ask for no better window into human nature than to work in one of the numerous chapels that dot the Vegas landscape.

In addition to a variety of traditional chapels, you can choose to tie the knot at a drive-though window, or even order a minister and attendants as a "Weddings-To-Go" delivery, much as you might order a pizza! Valentine's Day is an especially popular day to tie the knot in Vegas: In an average year, over 25,000 couples tie the knot there on February 14. Below are stories and quotes from some friendly people who work in the wedding industry in the most famous marriage destination of all.

What's the strangest thing you've seen lately?

"We had a whole group of people ride up to the drive-through window, and the bride and groom were in costumes—well, they all were! I don't remember what the bride was, but the groom was a Teletubby™. Oh, I just remembered, the bride was a chipmunk! And did I mention both of them and the whole wedding party was on mopeds? Believe me, it's not every day you marry someone in a Teletubby costume on a moped!"

"I think the strangest thing would have to be the bride who came in wearing a lovely traditional dress, and then before the ceremony she said that she had a little surprise for the groom, and she proceeded to strip down to a string bikini—and let me say, she might as well have been naked for all the coverage this bikini gave her—and the groom and the minister and the photographer were all shocked. Why, their mouths dropped open—they didn't expect it at all!"

What's the most romantic story you've seen?

"On Valentine's Day, I officiated at a wedding that was definitely the most romantic story I know. It was an older couple, and their daughter was with them. She told me the story, how her mother and father had met and dated during World War II, and then he was shipped out and they never saw each other again, even though it turned out she was pregnant! But because of some miscommunication, she believed the father of her baby had died in the war, and meanwhile he was at war and couldn't get through to her and finally assumed she had dumped him, all the while not knowing he had a baby daughter. After the war, she met someone else and married him, and whenever the daughter asked about her birth father, the mother just told her he died in the war, but the daughter never really believed that was true. So when the daughter was grown up, and was married herself, she set out to find her father. By this time her mother's husband had died so she was a widow. And it turned out the father was alive, and he had married but his wife had died, so he was a widower, and as soon as the two long-ago lovers were reunited, they decided to finally get married after all those years apart, and I married them."

What are some unusual locations for the Weddings-To-Go service?

"We recently had a wedding in a parking structure. It was for a couple from Finland, and apparently their two families owned several of the largest parking lots in Finland, and they wanted to honor the family businesses by getting married in one in Las Vegas. We closed off a whole area of a parking structure, and they had an Elvis impersonator, lots of streamers and decorations, and a gospel choir. It was quite a lovely wedding, actually."

Ever have anyone back out at the last minute, right at the altar?

"Nope, never in the six years I've been working here."

"No, but I have heard of it happening to other people."

"I think before I started working here I heard a few stories. . . never seen it myself."

What's the most promising couple you've married?

"I think it was the couple where the groom had had a heart transplant and the bride had been through several other surgeries, and they both held on to their health and recovered so that they could marry."

What's the least promising couple you've married?

"That would probably be this couple I had recently, where he was a 38-year-old man and she was sixteen. It was definitely a father-figure

type relationship, and I don't give it very long.
. . . In fact, I'd be surprised if they're still married now."

Special thanks to Little Church of the West, The Chapel of Love, and A Special Memory chapel. If you have a hankering to get hitched in Vegas, give these fine people a call.

Little Church of the West
4617 S. Las Vegas Blvd.
Las Vegas, NV 89119
702-739-7971 or 800-821-2452

Chapel of Love
1431 S. Las Vegas Blvd.
Las Vegas, NV 89104
702-387-0155 or 800-922-5683

A Special Memory Wedding Chapel
800 S. 4th St.
Las Vegas, NV 89101
702-384-2211 or 800-962-7798

NOTEWORTHY LAS VEGAS MARRIAGES:

Elvis and Priscilla Presley

Frank Sinatra and Mia Farrow

Jane Fonda and Roger Vadim

Bruce Willis and Demi Moore

Cindy Crawford and Richard Gere

Paul Newman and Joanne Woodward

Steve Lawrence and Eydie Gorme

Ann-Margret and Roger Smith

Brigitte Bardot

Joan Collins

Judy Garland

Vic Damone

Tony Curtis

Mickey Rooney and Ava Gardner

Mickey Rooney (seven more times)

Mary Tyler Moore

Sammy Davis Jr.

Bing Crosby

Joan Crawford

Michael Jordan

Dennis Rodman and Carmen Electra

Greg Allman

Shirley Bassey

David Cassidy

Bob Geldof

Zsa Zsa Gabor and George Sanders

Betty Grable and Harry James

Dudley Moore

Jon Bon Jovi

Mansfield Park

By Jane Austen

It was a very proper wedding. The bride was elegantly dressed; the two bridesmaids were duly inferior; her father gave her away; her mother stood with salts in her hand, expecting to be agitated; her aunt tried to cry; and the service was impressively read by Dr. Grant. Nothing could be objected to when it came under the discussion of the neighbourhood, except that the carriage which conveyed the bride and bridegroom and Julia from the church-door to Sotherton was the same chaise which Mr. Rushworth had used for a twelvemonth before. In everything else the etiquette of the day might stand the strictest investigation.

BEST MOVIE AND TV WEDDINGS

MOVIES

Philadelphia Story (1940)

The classic best-ever wedding scene, for when true love takes a while to be recognized. And don't miss *High Society* (1956), the musical version of *Philadelphia Story*, featuring Cole Porter tunes and Louis Armstrong's band!

Four Weddings and a Funeral (1994)

Like the title says, weddings and more weddings. Two wedding guests keep running into each other at the weddings of their friends. Will they get together themselves in the end?

Monsoon Wedding (2001)

The title wedding is a lovely affair, but the secondary wedding at the end is even more romantic.

Like Water for Chocolate (1992)

Not your typical wedding scene, since Tita, the true love of the groom Pedro, has to watch him marry her sister.

Father of the Bride (1950)

The Spencer Tracy version of course, although the Steve Martin remake isn't bad. Watch what happens as a father enters the "Wedding Planet," where he deals with all the planning involved with marrying off his beloved daughter.

TV

Some of the most popular shows on the small screen were those that featured weddings. Who can forget:

Luke and Laura's wedding on *General Hospital*: The whole country tuned in to see the popular daytime soap celebrate characters Luke and Laura's much-hyped nuptials in 1981.

Pride and Prejudice: The tangled web that must be unraveled before Elizabeth and her Mr. Darcy can live happily ever after made it a wedding worth waiting for on the popular BBC miniseries.

Mike and Gloria on *All in the Family*: When they finally tied the knot, it was a standout episode of this long-running 1970s sitcom.

THROWING RICE

Rice has long been considered a symbol of fertility and long life, so it entered popular wedding culture as a way for guests to express their good wishes to the newly married couple. Guests throw it at the bride and groom as a wish for children and a good life.

Because it was sometimes thought that birds would come along and eat the discarded rice, which was bad for their delicate bodies, some well-wishers have switched to throwing birdseed or sometimes paper confetti in lieu of rice as a post-wedding "shower" for the couple. Other good-luck charms that might be tossed are orange blossoms, corn, barley, chickpeas, or dates and figs to sweeten the marriage.

When two people are under the influence of the most violent, most insane, most delusive, and most transient of passions, they are required to swear that they will remain in that excited, abnormal, and exhausting condition continuously until death do them part.

—George Bernard Shaw

THE STORY OF THE HONEYMOON

The moon has always symbolized the organizing of time; even the very word "month" has its root in "moon." One theory of why we have the word "honeymoon" is that the first month of a couple's marriage was a "month as sweet as honey."

However, a more widely accepted derivation of the term "honeymoon" is that the Scandinavian and Teutonic people began the practice of the "honeymoon" in ancient times. Their wedding ceremonies were only held under the full moon, and then after the wedding, the bride and groom would drink honey wine for one full moon cycle (thirty days) after their wedding day. This first month of married life became known as the "honey moon."

While the name survived, the purpose of the honeymoon changed. After the wedding, newlyweds would leave their family and friends to go and do what newlyweds are supposed to do (nudge nudge, wink wink). Today the custom survives, only now a vacation is incorporated. The honeymoon is usually to a romantic getaway locale, and unfortunately it rarely lasts a whole month!

Our Deportment

BY JOHN H. YOUNG, A.M.

In the following excerpts from his 1879 book, Mr. Young states in no uncertain terms that the husband and wife must follow very specific roles in a marriage. The wife should "never indulge in fits of temper, hysterics, or other habits of ill-breeding" and yet, even if she does, the husband "should never seek to break her of any disagreeable habits or peculiarities she may possess, by ridiculing them."

CONDUCT OF HUSBAND AND WIFE

Let neither ever deceive the other, or do anything to shake the other's confidence, for once deceived, the heart can never wholly trust again. Fault-finding should only be done by gentle and mild criticism, and then with loving words and pleasant looks. Make allowances for one another's weaknesses, and at the same time endeavor to mutually repress them. For the sake of mutual improvement the husband and wife should receive and give corrections to one another in a spirit of kindness, and in doing so they will prepare themselves for the work God gives the parents of training lives for usefulness here and hereafter. Their motto should be "faithful unto death in all things," and they must exercise forbearance with each other's peculiarities.

A MISTAKEN MARRIAGE

If, perchance, after they have entered upon the stern realities of life, they find that they have made a mistake, that they are not well mated, then they must accept the inevitable and endure to the end, "for better or for worse;" for only in this way can they find consolation for having found out, when too late, that they were unfitted for a life-long companionship. A journalist has said: "No lessons learned by experience, however sharply taught and sadly earned, can enlighten the numbed senses which love has sent to sleep by its magic fascination; and things as plain as the sun in heaven, to others are dark as night, unfathomable as the sea, to those who let themselves love before they prove."

DUTIES OF THE WIFE TO HER HUSBAND

The wife should remember that upon her, to the greatest extent, devolves the duty of making home happy. She should do nothing to make her husband feel uncomfortable, either mentally or physically, but on the other hand she should strive to the utmost of her ability to do whatever is best calculated to please him, continually showing him that her love, plighted upon the altar, remains steadfast, and that no vicissitudes of fortune can change or diminish it. She should never indulge in fits of temper, hysterics, or other habits of ill-breeding, which, though easy to conquer at first, grow and strengthen with indulgence, if she would retain her husband as her lover and her dearest and nearest friend. She should be equally as neat and tidy respecting her dress and personal appearance at home as when she appears in society, and her manners toward her husband should be as kind and pleasing when alone with him as when in company.

A HUSBAND'S DUTIES

It is the husband's duty to join with his wife in all her endeavors to instruct her children, to defer all matters pertaining to their discipline to her, aiding her in this respect as she requires it. In household matters the wife rules predominant, and he should never interfere with her authority and government in this sphere. It is his duty and should be his pleasure to accompany her to church, to social gatherings, to lectures and such places of entertainment as they both mutually enjoy and appreciate. In fact he ought not to attend a social gathering unless accompanied by his wife, nor go to an evening entertainment without her. If it is not a fit place for his wife to attend, neither is it fit for him.

While he should give his wife his perfect confidence in her faithfulness, trusting implicitly to her honor at all times and in all places, he should, on his part, remain faithful and constant to her, and give her no cause of complaint. He should never seek to break her of any disagreeable habits or peculiarities she may possess, by ridiculing them. He should encourage her in all her schemes for promoting the welfare of her household, or in laudable endeavors to promote the happiness of others, by engaging in such works of benevolence and charity as the duties of her home will allow her to perform.

The husband, in fact, should act toward his wife as becomes a perfect gentleman, regarding her as the "best lady in the land," to whom, above all other earthly beings, he owes paramount allegiance.

One advantage of marriage, it seems to me, is that when you fall out of love with him or he falls out of love with you, it keeps you together until maybe you fall in again.

—Judith Viorst

ANNIVERSARY GIFTS

The practice of giving specific gifts on various wedding anniversaries originated in Central Europe. Among the medieval Germans it was customary for a wreath of silver to be given to a woman when she had lived with her husband for twenty-five years. The silver symbolized the harmony required for such a long-lived union. On the fiftieth anniversary of a wedding, the wife was presented with a similar wreath as before, only this time made out of gold.

From this tradition, we get the phrases "silver wedding" and "golden wedding." In modern times, other annual gift items were devised to have similar symbolic value to a married couple celebrating their years together.

YEAR	TRADITIONAL GIFT
1st	Paper
2nd	Cotton
3rd	Leather
4th	Linen, silk
5th	Wood
6th	Iron
7th	Wool, copper
8th	Bronze
9th	Pottery, china
10th	Tin, aluminum
11th	Steel
12th	Silk
13th	Lace
14th	Ivory (now banned)
15th	Crystal
20th	China
25th	Silver
30th	Pearl
35th	Coral

YEAR	TRADITIONAL GIFT
40th	Ruby
45th	Sapphire
50th	Gold
55th	Emerald
60th	Diamond
75th	Diamonds, gold

Somewhere along the line, retailers came to the conclusion that such formal traditions might be limiting the buying habits of the public, so the anniversary gift "traditions" were widened to include appliances, desk sets, and more.

The "odd years" between major milestones are also filled in, so now you'll know that for your dear friends' 29th anniversary, you should buy them new furniture, not to be confused with their 28th anniversary, when you should thoughtfully buy them orchids.

YEAR	MODERN GIFT	YEAR	MODERN GIFT
1st	Clock	15th	Watches
2nd	China	16th	Silver hollowware
3rd	Crystal, glass	17th	Furniture
4th	Electrical appliances	18th	Porcelain
5th	Silverware	19th	Bronze
6th	Wood	20th	Platinum
7th	Desk sets, pen and pencil sets	21st	Brass, nickel
8th	Linen, Lace	22nd	Copper
9th	Leather	23rd	Silver plate
10th	Diamonds, jewelry	24th	Musical instruments
11th	Fashion jewelry, accessories	25th	Sterling silver
12th	Pearls, colored gems	26th	Original pictures
13th	Textiles, furs	27th	Sculpture
14th	Gold, jewelry	28th	Orchids
		29th	New furniture
		30th	Diamond

YEAR	MODERN GIFT	YEAR	MODERN GIFT
31st	Timepieces	47th	Books
32nd	Conveyances	48th	Optical goods
33rd	Amethyst	49th	Luxury items
34th	Opal	50th	Gold
35th	Jade	55th	Emerald
36th	Bone china	60th	Diamond
37th	Alabaster	75th	Diamonds, gold
38th	Beryl, tourmaline		
39th	Lace		
40th	Ruby		
41st	Land		
42nd	Improved real estate		
43rd	Travel		
44th	Groceries		
45th	Sapphire		
46th	Original poetry tribute		

Life has taught me that love does not consist of gazing at each other but looking together in the same direction.

—Antoine de St. Exupery

CHAPTER IV

Making Love

O to draw you to me, to plant on you for the first time the lips of a determin'd man.
—Walt Whitman

Take a walk on the erotic side of love, as you read this chapter devoted to the art of making love. From classic poetry to modern novels, writers have always celebrated the physical aspects of love, and the excerpts found in this chapter range from the sensual poetry of Whitman and Cavafy to the surprisingly raw prose of the infamous eighteenth-century novel, *Fanny Hill* (you must be eighteen to read it!). In addition, explore highlights from what is perhaps the most well-known sex manual in the world, The *Kama Sutra*, written in ancient times to introduce lovers to the art of human sexuality, and translated and reprinted for centuries.

Jumping forward to more modern sex scenes, check out a list of steamy movies to rent, complete with synopses and descriptions of erotic scenes. And when you're ready for some steamy action of your own, don't forget to consult the list of aphrodisiacs, as well as a brief tutorial on male and female erogenous zones. Finally, you'll discover a few simple recipes for dinner and dessert, especially for lovers, and even suggestions on what to pack for the perfect romantic picnic.

When They Come Alive

BY CONSTANTINE CAVAFY

Try to keep them, poet,
those erotic visions of yours,
however few of them there are that can
*   be stilled.*
Put them, half-hidden, in your lines.
Try to hold them, poet,
when they come alive in your mind
at night or in the noonday brightness.

FUN FACT! The average person spends a total of two weeks kissing in an entire lifetime.

Steamy Movies to Rent

Here's a short list of films to pick up at the video store next time you're in the mood for something a little . . . adult (but you don't want pornography!). These films manage to walk the fine line between sensual and downright dirty.

Body Heat (1981)

In this sexy thriller, Matty (Kathleen Turner) seduces Ned (William Hurt). It's hard to decide which is hotter: the Florida heat wave in which the film is set, or the sweaty, sexy action between the two stars.

Wild Orchid (1990)

James Wheeler (Mickey Rourke) is a Machiavellian millionaire looking for some kinky sex, and naïve young lawyer Emily (Carré Otis) falls under his spell.

Showgirls (1995)

File this one under so-bad-it's-good. This ridiculous drama tries to blow the lid off the steamy underworld of strip clubs, but instead is so tacky it will amaze and delight you.

Two Girls and a Guy (1997)

In this mostly improvised drama, a two-timing cad (Robert Downey Jr.) fights and makes up with both of his girlfriends, and ooh, nothing gets a couple more revved up than a good fight!

Wild Things (1998)

This film features a ménage-à-trois between Denise Richards, Neve Campbell, and Matt Dillon that just about steams up the screen as you watch it.

Ghost (1990)

This drama is not a sexy movie in general, but there is one notable scene with clay that's often listed in movie fans' lists of top movie sex scenes, even though no clothing ever comes off—that's how hot it is!

ALSO . . .

Check out your local video store for adult-themed anime (Japanese animation). *The Sakura Diaries* (four volumes, released in 1999 and 2000) are a good place to start.

Russ Meyer is a director not to be missed! *Beyond the Valley of the Dolls* (1970) is a classic, and all of his films of the '60s and '70s are a treat, filled with busty heroines who let it all hang out.

One Hour to Madness and Joy
BY WALT WHITMAN

*One hour to madness and joy! O furious! O
    confine me not!*

(What is this that frees me so in storms?

*What do my shouts amid lightnings and raging
    winds mean?)*

*O to drink the mystic deliria deeper than any
    other man!*

*O savage and tender achings! (I bequeath them
    to you my children,*

*I tell them to you, for reasons, O bridegroom
    and bride.)*

*O to be yielded to you whoever you are, and you
to be yielded to me in defiance of the world!*

O to return to Paradise! O bashful and feminine!

O to draw you to me, to plant on you for the
first time the lips of a determin'd man.

O the puzzle, the thrice-tied knot, the deep
and dark pool, all untied and illumin'd!
O to speed where there is space enough and
air enough at last!
To be absolv'd from previous ties and conven
tions, I from mine and you from yours!
To find a new unthought-of nonchalance with
the best of Nature!
To have the gag remov'd from one's mouth!
To have the feeling to-day or any day I am
sufficient as I am.

O something unprov'd! something in a trance!
To escape utterly from others' anchors and holds!
To drive free! to love free! to dash reckless and
dangerous!

To court destruction with taunts, with invitations!
To ascend, to leap to the heavens of the love
*   indicated to me!*
To rise thither with my inebriate soul!
To be lost if it must be so!
To feed the remainder of life with one hour of
*   fullness and freedom!*
With one brief hour of madness and joy. 🙚

FUN FACT ! According to a national survey, fifty-six percent of men have had sex while at work.

EROGENOUS ZONES

Below, some spots on their bodies that men and women find especially sensitive, and they're not always the same for the different genders. Leaving aside the obvious, here are a few places to consider stimulating next time you want to try something new.

Of course all women are different, but many report being especially turned on when attention is paid to the following:

Neck: Kissing her neck while you play with her hair is good.

Buttocks: Squeezing and even a gentle spanking is sometimes welcome.

Inner thigh: Gentle kissing and licking can drive some women crazy with desire.

Feet: A nice foot rub feels great and is very relaxing.

Back: Whether massaging or lightly scratching, most women love their backs to be attended to.

Many people think men's erogenous zones are simply their sexual organs, but don't neglect these areas:

Lips: Kissing and even nibbling the lips can be a big turn on for many men.

Nipples: Many women assume men's nipples aren't very sensitive, which is just plain wrong.

Buttocks: Squeezing, spanking, whatever feels right.

Hair/Scalp: Many men enjoy having their hair ruffled and scalp massaged.

Back of knees: This sensitive body part is ticklish, so be careful.

FUN FACT! Approximately one hundred million acts of sexual intercourse occur around the world each day, according to a World Health Organization statistic.

Sucking Cider Through a Straw

BY ANONYMOUS

The prettiest girl
That ever I saw
Was sucking cider
through a straw.

I told that girl
I didn't see how
She sucked the cider
Through the straw.

And cheek by cheek
And jaw by jaw
We sucked that cider
through that straw.

And all at once
That straw did slip;

I sucked some cider
From her lip.

And now I've got
Me a mother-in-law
From sucking cider
Through a straw.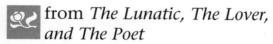

from *The Lunatic, The Lover, and The Poet*

BY MYRLIN HERMES

Midsummer night and here is his dream. She is lying back in bed, black hair undone and long, and wherever her hair is not, her nakedness. And he does not know which of these affects him more, the hair, or the nakedness. Or the way her lips close around the stem of her hammered silver pipe. The pipe has been worked by a fine and nimble hand to resemble the scales of a snake, the shallow bowl set with two gem-stones for the serpent's eyes. The tip is tapered, so the slimmer end rests neatly in the gap between her teeth. Horatio likes the fit of it—the way it invites the eye into her very mouth, revealing there the slightest hint of what might lie inside.

Her smell, clinging and everywhere, teases him. He does not know why this should be so—it is not a delightful odor which sends him into such prurient obsession. She reeks of autumn: overripe fruit and musk, decay and bonfire. Her breath is sour with wine and sweet with the rare blend of black tobacco she prefers, which she keeps in a sandalwood box beside the bed. Imported not from the New

World but the far reaches of the Old, its smoke is permeated with the scent of the exotic spices and perfumes which shared its long journey from the Orient.

He marvels at a woman's body—so much smaller than a man's! He might gather it up into his arms, the way he gathers her hair up to kiss her neck, then lets it spill down over those delicate shoulders. How narrow she is! And yet possessed of depths which enclose him; and others which he may never hope to penetrate. Though he has closed himself around the prince as fingers clasped in prayer, she uncloses him, slowly opening herself.

"Tell me about him," she whispers. "Tell me everything."

And he does. He tells her everything he has known with the prince, repeating Hamlet's cruel words and his crazy words and sweet. Embracing one another, Hamlet is the third, invisible, embraced in the space between them. Until suddenly, there is no space between them at all; not enough to dance on the head of a pin.

And as her ravenous mouth spreads and widens his own, he tastes in the pungent odor of her breath the smoke of her pipe and the Oriental spices, and the exotic dust of their journey, ten thousand miles or more, in slow gypsy caravans. And he is traveling with them, along paths more ancient than his beloved Ancients, on roadways never built by Man, but cleft, like canyons, by his feet in the earth.

Something in him breaks—like a looking-glass breaks, or like a wave—and he clenches his teeth to keep from crying aloud. As his eyes flutter shut, he calls on Heaven, and sees the prince's face. 🌺

This excerpt is from Myrlin Hermes' new book, a surreal work of Shakespearean scholarship. She is the author of Careful What You Wish For *(Simon & Schuster, 1999).*

FUN FACT! Scientific studies show that the following odors can increase blood flow to the penis: lavender, licorice, chocolate, doughnuts, pumpkin pie.

APHRODISIACS
THROUGH THE AGES

The dictionary defines "aphrodisiac" as "an agent, usually a food or drug, that arouses or is held to arouse sexual desire." Interestingly, the original definition of the Greek word *aphrodisiakos* was "a gem containing sexual powers." But since eating and sex have so often been linked together as sensual pleasures, it is no surprise that the usage of the term throughout recorded history soon came to refer to certain foods and recipes held to have special powers to excite lovers.

Scores of folk wisdom about aphrodisiacs have been passed from generation to generation. Ancient Arabic texts refer to such concoctions as "a glass of thick honey, twenty almonds, and one-hundred pine nuts," a rather thick-sounding cocktail that was to be drunk at bedtime for three nights in a row to increase sexual pleasure. In medieval Europe, plants that resembled the male sex organ were said to have special powers, so cucumbers, mushrooms, and certain root vegetables were much prized by lovers cooking a special meal. In ancient China, powders and oils were mixed together scientifically to create medicinal potions for lovers. They used such ingredients as ground deer horns and animal livers.

In modern times, the following are thought to aid in desire and sexual satisfaction: strawberries, chocolate, coffee, and wine. Herbalists say that the ginseng root is a stimulant. Some scientists have shown that perfumes which contain extracts of human pheromones cause the wearer to be more sexually attractive to potential mates. And of course, any fine meal prepared with love is always a turn-on.

APHRODISIAC	REPUTED PROPERTY
Strawberries	Strawberries are traditionally thought to inspire lovers.
Chocolate	Supposedly chocolate mimics feelings of love and contentment in the brain.
Asparagus	People who eat a lot of asparagus are said to have many lovers.
Pomegranate	The pomegranate fruit was considered a sacred representation of Aphrodite, goddess of love.
Oysters	Oysters are said to be sexual stimulants, perhaps because of their smooth texture.
Roses	The scent of roses is always romantic, and believed to inspire sensual acts.

A LOVER'S PICNIC

Pack a bag or basket with cloth napkins, eating utensils, glasses, and plates.

Purchase the following items at a gourmet grocery store:

- several cheeses of your choice (brie is especially good, or other soft cheeses)
- crusty French bread
- fresh grapes, or other seasonal fruits
- dark chocolate
- (optional) a bottle of wine

Go to a park or other outdoor area suitable for a picnic.

Enjoy!

from *Song of Myself*
BY WALT WHITMAN

*I believe in you my soul, the other I am must
    not abase itself to you,
And you must not be abased to the other.*

*Loafe with me on the grass, loose the stop
    from your throat,
Not words, not music or rhyme I want, not
    custom or lecture, not even the best,
Only the lull I like, the hum of your valved
    voice.*

*I mind how once we lay such a transparent
    summer morning,
How you settled your head athwart my hips*

and gently turn'd over upon me,
And parted the shirt from my bosom-bone,
*   and plunged your tongue*
* to my bare-stript heart,*
And reach'd till you felt my beard, and
*   reach'd till you held my feet.*

Swiftly arose and spread around me the peace
*   and knowledge that pass*
all the argument of the earth,
And I know that the hand of God is the prom
*   ise of my own,*
And I know that the spirit of God is the brother
*   of my own,*
And that all the men ever born are also my
*   brothers, and the women*
my sisters and lovers,

And that a kelson of the creation is love,
And limitless are leaves stiff or drooping in
the fields,
And brown ants in the little wells beneath
them,
And mossy scabs of the worm fence, heap'd
stones, elder, mullein and poke-weed. 🍃

FUN FACT! The distance sperm travels to fertilize an egg is three to four inches. Based on the size of sperm, the equivalent distance for a person to travel would be 26 miles (in other words, a marathon!).

The Kama Sutra

Very little is known about the ancient Indian sage Vatsyayana, not even exactly when he lived. Estimates place him any time between 1000 and 3000 B.C. We do know this, however: He produced the first written record of the religious study known as *The Kama Sutra*, a guide on how people should pursue sexual and sensual pleasures—and why this is a pursuit worthy of dedicating to the gods!

Few people realize there is more to the book than simply sexual calisthenics. In fact, there are all sorts of rules for lovers, many of them sounding downright odd to modern ears. For instance, here is a tidbit from the section on how to have proper fights as man and wife: "During a fight, the wife is allowed to pull the husband's hair and kick him. However, she must remain in the room until given permission to leave."

The original work was not particularly explicit, but later generations added more sexual content and lavish color illustrations. In 1883, Sir William Burton wrote a definitive translation of the work, and since then, *The Kama Sutra* has famously been used as a marital aid in many cultures.

SEXUAL UNION

Vatsyayana divided men and women into categories depending on the size of their sexual organs. His definitions were as follows:

"MAN is divided into three classes, viz. the hare man, the bull man, and the horse man, according to the size of his lingam. WOMAN also, according to the depth of her yoni, is either a female deer, a mare, or a female elephant." He then has a chart showing which types of men and women are most compatible, and goes on to discuss in detail the best positions for sexual intercourse.

Here are a few of the positions in the book. But be sure to look for an illustrated version before trying these, and in many cases, it's enough just to read about them, since some positions seem like they wouldn't be very comfortable.

THE CONGRESS OF A COW

When a woman stands on her hands and feet like a quadruped, and her lover mounts her like a bull, it is called the "congress of a cow." At this time everything that is ordinarily done on the bosom should be done on the back.

In the same way can be carried on the congress of a dog, the congress of a goat, the congress of a deer, the forcible mounting of an ass, the congress of a cat, the jump of a tiger, the pressing of an elephant, the rubbing of a boar, and the mounting of a horse. And in all these cases the characteristics of these different animals should be manifested by acting like them.

THE CLASPING POSITION

When the legs of both the male and the female are stretched straight out over each other, it is called the "clasping position." It is of two kinds, the side position and the supine position, according to the way in which they lie down. In the side position the male should invariably lie on his left side, and cause the woman to lie on her right side, and this rule is to be observed in lying down with all kinds of women.

When, after congress has begun in the clasping position, the woman presses her lover with her thighs, it is called the "pressing position."

THE SPLITTING OF A BAMBOO

When the woman places one of her legs on her lover's shoulder, and stretches the other out, and then places the latter on his shoulder, and stretches out the other, and continues to do so alternately, it is called the "splitting of a bamboo."

FUN FACT! The first two sperm banks in the world opened in 1964, one in Japan (Tokyo) and one in the U.S. (Iowa City).

Fanny Hill, or Memoirs of a Woman of Pleasure

BY JOHN CLELAND, ©1749

We went down the back-stairs very softly, and opening the door of a dark closet, where there was some old furniture kept, and some cases of liquor, she drew me in after her, and fastening the door upon us, we had no light but what came through a long crevice in the partition between ours and the light closet, where the scene of action lay; so that sitting on those low cases, we could, with the greatest ease, as well as clearness, see all objects (ourselves unseen), only by applying our eyes close to the crevice, where the moulding of a panel had warped, or started a little on the other side.

The young gentleman was the first person I

saw, with his back directly towards me, looking at a print. Polly was not yet come: in less than a minute tho', the door opened, and she came in; and at the noise the door made he turned about, and came to meet her, with an air of the greatest tenderness and satisfaction.

After saluting her, he led her to a couch that fronted us, where they both sat down, and the young Genoese help'd her to a glass of wine, with some Naples bisket on a salver. Presently, when they had exchanged a few kisses, and questions in broken English on one side, he began to unbutton, and, in fine, stript to his shirt. As if this had been the signal agreed on for pulling off all their cloaths, a scheme which the heat of the season perfectly favoured, Polly began to draw her pins, and as she had no stays to unlace, she was in a trice, with her gallant's officious assistance, undress'd to all but her shift.

When he saw this, his breeches were immediately loosen'd, waist and knee bands, and slipped over his ankles, clean off; his shirt collar was unbuttoned too: then, first giving Polly an encouraging kiss, he stole, as it were, the shift off the girl, who being, I suppose, broke and familiariz'd to this humour, blush'd indeed, but less than I did at the apparition of her, now standing stark-naked, just as she came out of the hands of pure nature, with her black hair loose and a-float down her dazzling white neck and shoulders, whilst the deepen'd carnation of her cheeks went off gradually into the hue of glaz'd snow: for such were the blended tints and polish of her skin.

This girl could not be above eighteen: her face regular and sweet-featur'd, her shape exquisite; nor could I help envying her two ripe enchanting breasts, finely plump'd out in flesh, but withal so round, so firm, that they sustain'd themselves, in scorn of any stay: then their nipples, pointing different ways, mark'd their pleasing separation; beneath them lay the delicious tract of the belly, which terminated in a parting or rift scarce discernible, that modesty seem'd to retire downwards, and seek shelter between two plump fleshy thighs: the curling hair that overspread its delightful front, cloathed it with the richest sable fur in the universe: in short, she was evidently a subject for the painters to court her sitting to them for a pattern of female beauty, in all the true price and pomp of nakedness.

The young Italian (still in his shirt) stood gazing and transported at the sight of beauties that might have fir'd a dying hermit; his eager eyes devour'd her, as she shifted attitudes at his discretion: neither were his hands excluded their share of the high feast, but wander'd, on the hunt of pleasure, over every part and inch of her body, so qualified to afford the most exquisite sense of it.

In the mean time, one could not help observing the swell of his shirt before, that bolster'd out, and shewed the condition of things behind the curtain: but he soon remov'd it, by slipping his shirt over his head; and now, as to nakedness, they had nothing to reproach one another.

The young gentleman, by Phoebe's guess, was about two and twenty; tall and well limb'd. His body was finely form'd and of a most vigorous make, square-shoulder'd, and broad-chested: his face was not remarkable in any way, but for a nose inclining to the Roman, eyes large, black, and sparkling, and a ruddiness in his cheeks that was the more a grace, for his complexion was of the brownest, not of that dusky dun colour which excludes the idea of freshness, but of that clear, olive gloss which, glowing with life, dazzles perhaps less than fairness, and yet pleases more, when it pleases at all. His hair, being too short to tie, fell no lower than his neck, in short easy curls; and he had a few sprigs about his paps, that garnish'd his chest in a style of strength and manliness. Then his grand movement, which seem'd to rise out of a thicket of curling hair that spread from the root all round thighs and belly up to the navel, stood stiff and upright, but of a size to frighten me, by sympathy, for the small tender part which was the object of its fury, and which now lay expos'd to my fairest view; for he had, immediately on stripping off his shirt, gently push'd her down on the couch, which stood conveniently to break her willing fall. Her thighs were spread out to their utmost extension, and discovered between them the mark of the sex, the red-center'd cleft of flesh, whose lips, vermilioning inwards, exprest a small rubid line in sweet miniature, such as Guido's touch of colouring could never attain to the life or delicacy of.

By this time the young gentleman had changed her posture from lying breadth to length-wise on the couch: but her thighs were still spread, and the mark lay fair for him, who now kneeling between them, display'd to us a side-view of that fierce erect machine of his, which threaten'd no less than splitting the tender victim, who lay smiling at the uplifted stroke, nor seem'd to decline it. He looked upon his weapon himself with some pleasure, and guiding it with his hand to the inviting slit, drew aside the lips, and lodg'd it (after some thrusts, which Polly seem'd even to assist) about half way; but there it stuck, I suppose from its growing thickness: he draws it again, and just wetting it with spittle, re-enters, and with ease sheath'd it now up to the hilt, at which Polly gave a deep sigh, which was quite another tone than one of pain; he thrusts, she heaves, at first gently, and in a regular cadence; but presently the transport began to be too violent to observe any order or measure; their motions were too rapid, their kisses too fierce and fervent for nature to support such fury long: both seem'd to me out of themselves: their eyes darted fires: "Oh!. . . oh!. . . I can't bear it. . . It is too much. . . I die. . . I am going . . ." were Polly's expressions of extasy.

His joys were more silent; but soon broken murmurs, sighs heart-fetch'd, and at length a dispatching thrust, as if he would have forced himself up her body, and then motionless languor of all his limbs, all shewed that the die-away moment was come upon him; which she gave signs of joining with, by the wild throwing of her hands about, closing her eyes, and giving a deep sob, in which she seemed to expire in an agony of bliss. ❧

Recipes for Lovers

MIXED BERRY FRENCH TOAST

The main benefit of this breakfast recipe is that it is not only delicious, but also easy to prepare—so you can save your energy for more romantic pursuits.

Ingredients
   FOR TOAST:
   6 slices bread, any kind
   (Note: Jewish challah is an excellent choice, or use any kind of thickly sliced white bread)
   3 eggs
   ¼ cup milk
   ½ tsp. vanilla
   1 teaspoon orange zest
   2 tbsp. butter

FOR TOPPING:
Any variety jam or preserves
Fresh mixed berries are even better

Beat eggs, vanilla, and milk together in a large bowl. Grate orange zest into egg mixture.

Melt a small amount of butter in a skillet over medium-high heat. One slice at a time, dip each piece of bread in the egg mixture, turning to coat completely. Place slices of bread in skillet, as many as can fit easily without overlapping.

When bottom side is golden (usually just a few minutes, depending on your stove), lift with spatula, place a dab more butter in the pan, and turn bread over to cook the other side. Keep finished slices in a warm oven.

Serve with jam and fruit.

BASIL CHICKEN

This light and easy meal is perfect for a last-minute dinner guest. Serve with a green salad and warm bread.

Ingredients
    4 boneless skinless chicken breasts
    1 bunch of fresh basil, or 3 tablespoons dried
    ½ cup plain yogurt
    2 tbsp. bread crumbs
    1 tbsp. cornstarch
    Grated parmesan cheese, to taste
    Dashes of salt and pepper

Preheat oven to 350 degrees. Chop basil leaves into ribbons.

In a mixing bowl, combine yogurt, cornstarch, and basil. Place chicken breasts in a baking dish large enough so they are not overlapping. Spoon the yogurt-basil mixture on top of them.

Combine the bread crumbs and cheese in a separate bowl, and add salt and pepper to taste. Spoon crumbs on top of the chicken breasts.

Bake for 30 minutes, or until chicken is cooked all the way through.

DECADENT BROWNIES

These are sinfully rich and chocolatey. You can either make them as is, with the white chocolate ganache on top, or substitute some other topping like fruit preserves or a nut butter of your choice.

Ingredients
  1 cup butter
  4 squares unsweetened chocolate
  2 cups sugar
  4 eggs
  2 tsp. vanilla
  1½ cups all-purpose flour
  1 tsp. baking powder
  1 tsp. salt

FOR THE TOPPING:
1 cup white chocolate chips or shaved
white chocolate (premium imported
brand)
1 cup heavy whipping cream
2 cups premium chocolate chips
1 to 1½ cups chopped, toasted pecans

Preheat oven to 350 degrees. Prepare 9 by
13-inch baking pan by greasing with butter or
spraying with nonstick cooking spray. Melt
butter in a large saucepan. Over low heat add
unsweetened chocolate and stir until chocolate
is melted. Remove from heat, and mix in sugar
(in saucepan). Add eggs and vanilla, stir until
incorporated. Add flour, baking powder, and
salt and stir just till flour is mixed in. Gently
stir in white chocolate. Spread mixture in prepared pan. Bake 30 to 35 minutes—just until

brownies begin to pull away from the sides. Remove from oven and let cool completely.

While brownies are baking, prepare ganache topping. Over low heat in a medium saucepan, bring heavy cream to the boil. Remove from heat and add chocolate chips. Let sit for a few minutes to melt chocolate. Stir until all chocolate is melted. Let mixture cool and thicken, stirring occasionally for about 20 to 30 minutes. Spread chocolate ganache over completely cooled brownies. Press chopped, toasted pecans into the ganache. Let ganache harden and then cut into squares and then into triangles. Carefully remove from pan and serve on a garnished plate.

ORANGE CHOCOLATE CHIP COOKIES

Beware, these are the most delicious cookies ever. Once you make them, you will have complete power over anyone who eats one.

Ingredients
- ½ cup butter, softened
- ⅓ cup packed brown sugar
- ⅓ cup white sugar
- 1 egg
- 1½ tsp. hot water
- 1⅛ cups all-purpose flour
- ½ tsp. orange extract
- ½ tsp. vanilla extract
- ½ tsp. baking soda
- ½ tsp. salt
- ½ cup semisweet chocolate chips
- 1 Droste® or other brand dark chocolate orange, cut into chip-size pieces*

Preheat oven to 375 degrees. Beat butter, brown sugar, granulated sugar, and egg until light and fluffy, about 3 minutes. Beat in hot water and extracts. Gradually beat in flour, baking soda, and salt, until well blended and smooth. Stir in chocolate chips and orange chocolate pieces.

Drop dough by well-rounded teaspoons onto greased cookie sheets. Bake for 10 minutes, or until golden. Cool cookie sheet on a wire rack for 1 minute, then remove cookies to a rack to cool completely.

*It is easiest to chop up the chocolate orange if it is frozen first. Stick the whole chocolate in the freezer for a day before using, if you have time.

CHAPTER V

Losing Love

She said to herself that perhaps he would come back to tell her he had not meant what he said; and she listened for his ring at the door, trying to believe that this was probable. A long time passed, but Morris remained absent.

—Henry James

This chapter looks at the darker side of romantic love. From literary scenes and quotes to personal anecdotes, this section is brimming with suggestions for healing a broken heart, or at the very least, offers proof that you're not the first person in the world to feel the pain of love's end.

Enjoy excerpts from Victorian melodrama, and sigh mournfully along with heroines from great novels. Don't miss the collection of bad dates, gathered from a variety of sources, all of whom had one thing in common: a willingness to share the most pathetic and uncomfortable pages from their dating diaries.

There is also a list of movies about divorce, and a suggested soundtrack for moping about lost love. You'll even find a list of some "light" reading about breakups and divorce, as many novelists have written warm, engaging stories centered on the dissolution of a marriage. Enjoy perusing a list of country song titles that say more about breakups in a few well-chosen words than whole libraries. And remember, just when you think it's hopeless, love will enter your life again.

> *We are never so helplessly unhappy as when we lose love.*
>
> *—Sigmund Freud*

 *Love's Pains*
BY JOHN CLARE

This love, I canna' bear it,
It cheats me night and day;
This love, I canna' wear it,
It takes my peace away.

This love, wa' once a flower;
But now it is a thorn—
The joy o' evening hour,
Turn'd to a pain e're morn.

This love, it wa' a bud,
And a secret known to me;
Like a flower within a wood;
Like a nest within a tree.

This love, wrong understood,
Oft' turned my joy to pain;
I tried to throw away the bud,
But the blossom would remain. 🌹

BAD DATES:
TALES FROM THE TRENCHES

THE HARRASSER

I was walking my dog in the park one day, and a cute guy came up and started chatting with me. Now, I generally am quite suspicious of strangers, but I had recently been told by several friends of mine that I needed to be more trusting and to believe in the possibility of romance, and he looked familiar. I guess I had seen him at the local café several times. So instead of politely excusing myself, I stayed and chatted, and agreed to meet him for coffee the following morning at the local Starbucks. We arranged a time, and I went home, feeling hopeful that perhaps I had finally met a decent guy.

The next morning, I arrived at the café at the appointed time. I got coffee and sat down to wait. Before long, my new friend walked in, but instead of sitting down with me, he was immediately accosted by the counter person, who said, "Excuse me sir, you're going to have to leave or I'm calling the police!" He gave me a look and a shrug that said, "I'd love to stay, but I can't," as he was escorted out of the place.

Naturally, I immediately went up to the counter and asked for the story. Turns out, the guy had been harassing the wait staff there, and the manager had told him he was no longer allowed in the place. I hid out in Starbucks for a long time, until I was sure he was no longer outside, and I rushed home, determined never to accept a date with a random stranger again.

As soon as I got home from the aborted date

and swung the door open, the phone was ringing. Yup. I had unfortunately given him my number, and he was calling. And calling. And calling. I screened calls for days. He kept calling. Nearly changed my number. At last the phoning stopped. Why, you ask?

Well, as it happened, the following week, I turned on the TV and caught the tail end of a news story where my Starbucks "date" was being led off in handcuffs. The news cut to a commercial break. I never did find out the meaning of that footage, but the bottom line is, I haven't seen him around again, and I haven't chatted up any more cute guys while walking my dog.

—Madison Clell

Madison Clell is a writer and comics artist; find her online at www.cuckoocomic.com.

THE CRYING MAN

The worst date I ever went on was the blind date with the guy who cried the whole way through dinner because his girlfriend had left him four days before. I don't think he was ready to be dating yet.

—Nancy Barrett

ENDLESS FERRY RIDE

This guy asked what I wanted to do on our first date, gave some options (which I always like), and I chose riding the Staten Island ferry. Well, the guy was *so happy*. When we met he just kept talking about how New York City women only want to get men to spend a lot of money on them and it was so refreshing that I actually wanted to ride the ferry instead of going out to a fancy restaurant. Well, I'd kinda hoped that *eventually* there would be food, but he just wanted to ride the ferry, back and forth, all night. Even if we were to go Dutch on dinner—Nah, wasn't it more *fun* to ride the ferry? This was all set to a monologue about how much everything cost in NYC. I should add—this guy was an attorney in a big white-shoe law firm, not a graffiti artist! Finally, I bought my own soda on the ferry—I got Coke rather than Diet Coke because I figured it was the only calories I was gonna get that night!

After like six round-trips, him doing all the talking (and complaining about women and expenses), I said, "Okay, I'm going home!" and he got all disappointed—Let's ride back to

Staten Island a few more times! He called for another date a couple of times after that. I never could figure out how to say I need more than Coca-Cola to survive.

—Ingrid Day

THE MUFFIN INCIDENT

I went out with this guy for about a month, and we realized it wasn't going to work out, so we parted. I realized just how true the "not working out" thing was the next time I saw him. He was arm-in-arm with an attractive man, and as I walked by, I heard him say to his friend, "Thanks, muffin!" I don't know which was more of a shock to me: that he was gay, or that he would actually call his lover "muffin"!

—Rita Tannenbaum

THE BATH-OBSESSED BANK TELLER

I went to the bank once and got this really cute teller. We started flirting, and he asked if we could get together for coffee or something. I'd just recently broken up with the love of my life and figured oh hell, why not? We set a date, and he asked if I could come to his place and pick him up. I did, although I wondered about that.

After I arrived, we chit-chatted a bit and as I was wondering when we would be leaving for wherever it was we were going, he asked, "So would you like to take a bath, now?" I'd already showered before coming over but he kept insisting until I said, "Why?! I just showered already, okay?" and he said oh no, no that he asked *all* his dates to take baths. I didn't stick around to hear why, as I was all b-bye! and heading out the door. My shortest date ever. Plus, it was annoying to have to go to another branch of that bank.

—Helen Keeler

THE LOST WALLET

I had arranged to meet a guy from a personal ad, named Bill, for coffee one afternoon. That morning, I had been about to run out to the store for groceries when I realized that my wallet was missing, and then realized it had been stolen the night before on a bus. I spent all morning calling and canceling credit cards, which the thieves were already using, filed a police report, did all the stuff you have to do in that situation. I had just enough scrounged change to get a bus over to meet Bill, but other than that, no money at all. Alas, all the nearby friends I called weren't

home. So off I set to meet him, apologizing pro-
fusely when I got there that I was late and had
no wallet and was having a horrible day and so
on. He was kind of scary looking, older than me
but with this weird bi-level haircut and leather
jacket like he was trying to look all cool and
youthful. Also really bad teeth. But nice, bought
me coffee, bought me lunch, bought me several
drinks at the Gypsy Lounge, drove me home and
by then I was pretty much plastered. I let him
help me up to my apartment, settled my head
on his lap sleepily and let him play with my hair
while we talked, all the while wondering how
the hell I was going to get out of this.

He was a gentleman, and when I said he'd
better go, he did. He called and emailed again,
and because I felt so guilty about the wallet
thing and sponging off him, I let myself be

talked into several more dates, but I never let him drive me home again, thereby avoiding the possible kissing thing. Eventually, I was busy several weekends in a row with out-of-town trips, and I told him I'd call when I got back to town in a few weeks, and just never did.

A year or so later, long after I had abandoned personal ads, I was idly trawling through some personals site and decided to answer a well-written ad. Naturally, it turned out to be Bill. He wrote me a cryptic reply saying "Perhaps you recall me, there was that lovely evening when you rested your head on my lap. I always liked you a lot and I'm sorry we fell out of touch, write back if you want to meet again." I think that was officially the *last* time I answered an ad. This town is just too small!

—Millie Waters

THE MUSIC LOVER

I had a date with a guy I met at a dance class, and after dinner we went back to his place and he asked if I liked music. I said yes, and turned to go look at his records and he popped out from behind the sofa with his accordion and started playing. *Loud. Folk songs of all nations.* He was really multitalented—that same evening he recited his toastmaster's "humorous" speech for me. He was a nice guy, but strangely, we never really "hit it off."

—Gidget

THE VASECTOMY GUY

His name was Ted. I had answered his personal ad in the local free newspaper, and we emailed back and forth a few times, and decided to meet for coffee. In his last email to me confirming the time and place, he mentioned proudly that he had had a vasectomy. That's an odd thing to tell someone you've never even met, I thought, but by then, the date was set. He arrived a few minutes after me, and he was carrying a large portfolio. He had told me he was a hobbyist photographer, but this was a little much, I thought, bringing his portfolio on a first date!

Okay, fine, I started to leaf through it at his suggestion, and all the photos were of women dressed like men! "I'm fascinated with androgyny," he told me. Fair enough, it's a fascinating subject, but the combination of the typical first-date jitters with the knowledge of his fascination with mannish women—plus the odd intimacy of knowing about his choice not to have children before we'd even ordered coffee—made me uncomfortable. To break the ice,

I suggested after we had our coffee we check out the old-fashioned game arcade across the street, a place I'd wanted to check out for ages but never had entered. He turned up his nose at the idea, saying he didn't like "that kind of thing." I was happy when a half-hour had passed and I could safely leave without seeming too rude.

—Jane Samiam

CRACKER BARREL BREAKFAST

I was set up with an "older gentleman" through a mutual friend, and after talking on the phone a few times, I met him for breakfast. He has a convertible, so his sporty cap seemed appropriate, as did his shorts, though I noticed there was sort of an incongruence between one part of the ensemble and the next. But not being a petty sort of person, I did not dwell. We zipped down the highway. ("I have a heavy foot, you'll notice," he said proudly and I pointed out the cop who had just pulled someone over, so ol' leadfoot lightened up.)

The restaurant he liked for breakfast turned out to be a Cracker Barrel; there was a thirty-minute wait, so we had a pleasant conversation and I was able to truly appreciate the gray silk shirt with the embroidered American Indian designs around cuff and hem, the green denim shorts, the white knee-highs with red and blue stripes around the top, the black sneakers. Cut quite a figure, I can assure you. But, not being a petty person, I did not dwell.

We had breakfast. Unlike some people, Bill was not coy about his age. Mentioned his honeymoon trip with his first wife in 1948, mentioned singing in the Hollywood Bowl in 1947, mentioned being a very young child in the early 1930s when men's bathing suits had to include a top. I'm not sure if he was trying to get me to say how old I was or just being straightforward. But while we got along fine, there was a certain avuncular nature to our interactions which was a tad unnerving, although perhaps inevitable.

After breakfast, we went to the Gypsy Caravan which is an annual fundraising event—a vast flea market. Too many people, too much sun, too little good stuff. We wandered about for an hour and decided we'd had enough. When he asked if I would mind if we left, I practically caroled "Oh, no!" and off we went. So he dropped me off by my car, then did a fast and loud U-turn and sped away.

—Karen Freeman

THE BAD BOY

I was on Christmas vacation during my first year in college, and my mom set me up with Reed, the mail-boy from her office. She swore up, down, and sideways that he was cool. He came over to the house to help us decorate the tree—there were about five of us there: him, me, my mother, and a couple of her friends. "Awkward" doesn't begin to describe it. I felt like I had suddenly stepped back into the '50s. The only thing that was missing was that he didn't have his hair shellacked to the sides of his head and wasn't wearing a reindeer sweater.

Like an idiot, I agreed to go to the movies with him the next day. So check it out: We're leaving the house, Mom is waving goodbye, and we get into the car, I turn to put on my seatbelt, and when I turn back to look at him, he's freakin' drinking from a flask. Behind the wheel of a car, with my Mom watching!

The best part was that when I looked at him like he'd grown a third eye in the middle of his forehead—a look I'd very carefully crafted to imply that drinking, let alone drinking and driving, in front of my mother's house when you're about to take her only child on a date is a bad idea—he said, "Oh, god, how rude of me. You want some?"

The date was pretty much over right then.

—Inger Klekacz

THE DOUBLE DATE

A boy I met from a different high school asked me out, but I didn't know him that well, so I suggested we double. I asked him to find a tall friend, since my friend was six feet tall. Well, his friend turned out to be about five-foot-two, squinty-eyed and nicknamed "Snake." My friend was less than pleased. They took us to see the movie *Scanners*, a truly bad horror flick in which people's heads explode with dismaying frequency. This, I believe, was meant to force my friend and me into the guys' arms or something. It didn't.

Later that evening we went down to the shore of Lake Michigan and walked out on a long grassy pier. My date lay down on the grass, and invited me to do the same. I was looking up at the stars, though, and was not really paying attention. I stepped backward, right onto his hand. I think I broke his pinkie. After they took us home very shortly thereafter, we never heard from either guy again.

—Kitt Beaulaire

Love is also like a coconut which is good while it is fresh, but you have to spit it out when the juice is gone; what's left tastes bitter.

—Bertolt Brecht

 When I Loved You

BY THOMAS MOORE

When I loved you, I can't but allow
I had many an exquisite minute;
But the scorn that I feel for you now
Hath even more luxury in it!

Thus whether we're on or we're off,
Some witchery seems to await you;
To love you is pleasant enough,
But oh! 'tis delicious to hate you!

MUSIC TO CRY BY

COUNTRY SONG MOURNIN'

These titles are but the tip of the iceberg. When it comes to love gone bad, country and honky-tonk songwriters wrote the book. Here is just a small selection of song titles to whet your appetite. Some suggested soundtracks for your breakup are in the following section (and not all country, either!).

"Another Somebody Done Somebody Wrong"

"Baby's Gotten Good at Goodbye"

"Dance With Who Brung You"

"Drivin' Nails in My Coffin"

"Eighteen Wheels and a Dozen Roses"

"Got No Reason Now for Going Home"

"Heartbroke"

"Here I Am Drunk Again"

"If We Make It Through December"

"I Love You So Much It Hurts"

"I Married Her Just Because She Looks Like You"

"I'm Only in It for the Love"

"Last Cheater's Waltz"

"May the Bird of Paradise Fly Up Your Nose"

"One Has My Name (The Other Has My Heart)"

"Remember Me) I'm the One Who Loves You"

"Someday (You'll Want Me to Want You)"

"Who Will Buy the Wine"

"You Never Even Call Me by My Name"

"You're the Reason God Made Oklahoma"

"You Two-Timed Me Once Too Often"

These songs hit the spot if your aim is to soothe your broken heart:

Patsy Cline: "Crazy," "I Fall to Pieces," "Sweet Dreams"

Willie Nelson: "Always on My Mind"

And a whole bushel of heartbreak in song from Hank Williams Sr., who recorded all of the following titles (and more!) to let you keep reliving the pain:

"Your Cheatin' Heart"

"Why Should We Try Anymore"

"I'm So Lonesome I Could Cry"

"Cold, Cold Heart"

"Long Gone Lonesome Blues"

"I Can't Help It (If I'm Still in Love With You)"

"I Can't Get You off of My Mind"

"Alone & Forsaken"

"Moanin' the Blues"

"Lovesick Blues"

"Weary Blues from Waitin'"

"They'll Never Take Her Love From Me"

"Take These Chains From My Heart"

THE TOP FIVE ALBUMS FOR MOPING

While breaking up is hard to do, there's no reason you shouldn't have a good soundtrack for it.

Frank Sinatra: *Sings For Only the Lonely* (1958)
Nine out of ten heartbroken people recommend this album! It may be the definitive breakup soundtrack. (It's a concept album about the end of a love affair, after all.)

Johnny Hartman and John Coltrane (1963)

This self-titled album is filled with jazz that is both haunting and sublime . . . music to sip your drink to and contemplate how it all went wrong.

Marvin Gaye: *Here, My Dear* (1978)

The legendary divorce album; a judge told Marvin to make a record and give his wife complete royalties. He recorded a wrenching, very specific double album tracing their relationship. Includes "When Did You Stop Loving Me, When Did I Stop Loving You."

Aretha Franklin: *Spirit in the Dark* (1970)

Aretha broke up with her abusive husband and wrote four songs for this album. During "The Thrill is Gone," she starts wailing "free at last!"; it's one of the most honest moments in recorded music.

Joni Mitchell: *Blue* (1971)

Sweet and sad and perfect for listening while you're curled up in bed, wondering how you ended up there.

Check these out for additional wallowing:

Nick Drake: *Pink Moon* (1972)

Beck: *Sea Change* (2002)

Damian Jurado: *Rehearsals For Departure* (1999)

Billy Strayhorn: *The Peaceful Side* (1961)

My Bloody Valentine: *Loveless* (1991)

Bob Mould: *Black Sheets of Rain* (1990)

The Smiths: *Singles* (1995)

Book of Love: *Lullaby* (1988)

Billy Bragg: *Workers Playtime* (1988)

Elvis Costello: *Blood & Chocolate* (1986)

Nick Cave: *From Her to Eternity* (1984)

Marianne Faithfull: *Blazing Away* (1990)

k.d. lang: *Ingénue* (1992)

Richard Thompson: *Shoot Out the Lights* (1982)

Richard Buckner: *Devotion + Doubt* (1997)

Sarah MacLachan: *Fumbling Towards Ecstasy* (1993)

Ani DiFranco: *Dilate* (1996)

Special thanks to Dan Buskirk, Rick Henderson, and the experts of genx who helped compile this list.

And if I loved you
Wednesday
So what if that is true
I do not love you
Thursday—
So much is true.

—Edna St. Vincent Millay

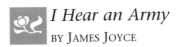 *I Hear an Army*
BY JAMES JOYCE

I hear an army charging upon the land,
And the thunder of horses plunging; foam
   about their knees:
Arrogant, in black armour, behind them stand,
Disdaining the reins, with fluttering whips, the
   Charioteers.

They cry into the night their battle name:
I moan in sleep when I hear afar their whirling
   laughter.
They cleave the gloom of dreams, a blinding
   flame,
Clanging, clanging upon the heart as upon an
   anvil.

*They come shaking in triumph their long grey
 hair:*
*They come out of the sea and run shouting by
 the shore.*
My heart, have you no wisdom thus to despair?
*My love, my love, my love, why have you left
 me alone?*

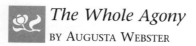

The Whole Agony
BY AUGUSTA WEBSTER

This monologue is from the Victorian melodrama *A
Woman Sold*, written in 1867. It captures the irony of
a broken heart, as the character of Lionel explains to
Eleanor, his former flame now betrothed to another,
that despite the pain of being rejected, he still loves
her.

Aye, if one could dissect one's living heart
And lecture coldly on it, I might speak
In sober phrases and set out my grief
With due pathetic touches, till perhaps
You'd weep a little for it. Now 'tis I
Who shed a fool's weak tears. Yes, keep your
    head
Turned from me; you are wise, for if you looked
You might remember, weren't but in a mood
Of foolish pity, that I am the man
Who trusted you, set all his hopes on you,
Because he had your promise, loved you past
All thought of treachery from you. Aye, there,
There in one breath is the whole agony,
I love you.

The Man and His Two Wives
BY AESOP

In the old days, when men were allowed to have many wives, a middle-aged Man had one wife that was old and one that was young; each loved him very much, and desired to see him like herself. Now the Man's hair was turning grey, which the young Wife did not like, as it made him look too old for her husband. So every night she used to comb his hair and pick out the white ones. But the elder Wife saw her husband growing grey with pleasure, for she did not like to be mistaken for his mother. So every morning she used to arrange his hair and pick out as many of the black ones as she could. The consequence was the Man soon found himself entirely bald.

Moral: Yield to all and you will soon have nothing to yield.

THE FACTS OF DIVORCE

We've all heard the old chestnut: "One out of every two marriages ends in divorce," but is that really true? According to the U.S. Census figures, maybe. The National Vital Statistics System reports on American marriage and divorce statistics annually, divided by region.

For example, in 1998, the New England states (Maine, New Hampshire, Vermont, Massachusetts, Rhode Island, and Connecticut) registered approximately 6,000 marriages and 3,000 divorces in the course of the year. But since those divorces happened to marriages formed prior to 1998, there is little correlation between the number of couples marrying in a year and the number of couples divorcing that same year.

However, there is enough numerical evidence of high divorce rates to suggest that the odds of a married couple staying together are slimmer today than they were in our grandparents' time. In fact, the National Center for Health Statistics recently released a report featuring this sad stat: 43 percent of first marriages end in separation or divorce within 15 years.

Since ther's no helpe . . .
BY MICHAEL DRAYTON

*Since ther's no helpe, Come let us kisse and
    part,*
Nay, I have done: You get no more of Me,
And I am glad, yea glad with all my heart,
That thus so cleanly, I my Selfe can free,
Shake hands for ever, Cancell all our Vowes,
And when We meet at any time againe,
Be it not seene in either of our Browes,
That We one jot of former Love reteyne;
Now at the last gaspe, of Loves latest Breath,
*When his Pulse fayling, Passion speechlesse
    lies,*
When Faith is kneeling by his bed of Death,
And Innocence is closing up his Eyes,

Now if thou would'st, when all have given
 him over,
From Death to Life, thou might'st him yet
 recover.

You Smiled, You Spoke
BY WALTER SAVAGE LANDOR

You smiled, you spoke and I believed,
By every word and smile—deceived.
Another man would hope no more;
Nor hope I—what I hoped before.

But let not this last wish be vain;
Deceive, deceive me once again!

Movies About Divorce

Kramer vs. Kramer (1979)

Dustin Hoffman and Meryl Streep are a divorced couple trying to navigate their shared parenthood.

Ordinary People (1980)

A broken family tries to heal after the death of the son and brother they loved. Donald Sutherland, Mary Tyler Moore, and Timothy Hutton star.

War of the Roses (1989)

A couple (Michael Douglas and Kathleen Turner) argues over who will keep their house in a vicious divorce battle.

The Parent Trap (1961)

Hayley Mills plays twins trying to get their

divorced parents to reunite in this children's classic.

Irreconcilable Differences (1984)

With her parents on the verge of divorce, Drew Barrymore plays their daughter who tries to divorce *them*!

His Girl Friday (1940)

This Howard Hawks comedy classic concerns an ex-husband (Cary Grant) who just can't bear to see his ex-wife (Rosalind Russell) remarry.

First Wives Club (1996)

Three women (Bette Midler, Goldie Hawn, and Diane Keaton), whose husbands each left them for younger women, band together to seek revenge, and end up doing good in the process.

When First I Met Thee
BY THOMAS MOORE

When first I met thee, warm and young,
There shone such truth about thee,
And on thy lip such promise hung,
I did not dare to doubt thee.
I saw thee change, yet still relied,
Still clung with hope the fonder,
And thought, though false to all beside,
From me thou couldst not wander.
But go, deceiver! go,
The heart, whose hopes could make it
Trust one so false, so low,
Deserves that thou shouldst break it.

When every tongue thy follies named,
I fled the unwelcome story,

Or found, in even the faults they blamed,
Some gleams of future glory.
I still was true, when nearer friends
Conspired to wrong, to slight thee;
The heart that now thy falsehood rends
Would then have bled to right thee.
But go, deceiver! go
Some day, perhaps, thou'lt waken
From pleasure's dream, to know
The grief of hearts forsaken.

Even now, though youth its bloom has shed,
No lights of age adorn thee;
The few who loved thee once have fled,
And they who flatter scorn thee.
Thy midnight cup is pledged to slaves,
No genial ties enwreath it;
The smiling there, like light on graves,

Has rank cold hearts beneath it.
Go—go—though worlds were thine,
I would not now surrender
One taintless tear of mine
For all thy guilty splendour!

And days may come, thou false one! yet,
When even those ties shall sever!
When thou wilt call, with vain regret,
On her thou'st lost for ever;
On her who, in thy fortune's fall,
With smiles had still received thee,
And gladly died to prove thee all
Her fancy first believed thee.
Go—go—'tis vain to curse,
'Tis weakness to upbraid thee;
Hate cannot wish thee worse
Than guilt and shame have made thee.

Washington Square
BY HENRY JAMES

In this moving scene, Catherine attempts to come to terms with the disappearance of Morris, the man she thought she would marry, who has told her he must leave town on business in such a way that she knows what he really means: He is throwing her over.

It was almost her last outbreak of passive grief; at least, she never indulged in another that the world knew anything about. But this one was long and terrible; she flung herself on the sofa and gave herself up to her misery. She hardly knew what had happened; ostensibly she had only had a difference with her lover, as other girls had had before, and the thing was not only not a rupture, but she was under no obligation to regard it even as a menace. Nevertheless, she felt a wound, even if he had not dealt it; it seemed to her that a mask had suddenly fallen from his face. He had wished to get away from her; he had been angry and cruel, and said strange things, with strange looks. She was smothered and stunned; she buried her head in the cushions, sobbing and talking to herself. But at last she raised herself, with the fear that either her father or Mrs. Penniman would come in; and then she sat there, staring before her, while the room grew darker. She said to herself that perhaps he would come back to tell her he had not meant what he said; and she listened for his ring at the door, trying to believe that this was probable.

A long time passed, but Morris remained absent; the shadows gathered; the evening settled down on the meagre elegance of the light, clear-coloured room; the fire went out. When it had grown dark, Catherine went to the window and looked out; she stood there for half an hour, on the mere chance that he would come up the steps. At last she turned away, for she saw her father come in. He had seen her at the window looking out, and he stopped a moment at the bottom of the white steps, and gravely, with an air of exaggerated courtesy, lifted his hat to her. The gesture was so incongruous to the condition she was in, this stately tribute of respect to a poor girl despised and forsaken was so out of place, that the thing gave her a kind of horror, and she hurried away to her room. It seemed to her that she had given Morris up. ✄

READING ABOUT DIVORCE

There are some novels and memoirs that describe the dissolution of a relationship without being inherently depressing.

Le Divorce, by Diane Johnson (1998)

This novel follows the adventures of Isabel Walker, a young attractive film-school dropout who moves to Paris to help her step-sister through a difficult divorce. If you enjoy this, be sure to check out her follow-up novel, *Le Mariage*!

Around the House and in the Garden: A Memoir of Heartbreak, Healing, and Home Improvement, by Dominique Browning (2002)

Browning, a former editor-in-chief of *House and Garden* magazine writes with warmth, humor, and insight about how she coped after a difficult divorce—by redecorating, of course!

About A Boy, by Nick Hornby (1998)

This charming novel features an unlikely friendship between Will, a terminal bachelor and Marcus, a twelve-year-old boy. Marcus turns to Will for help dealing with his divorced (and depressed) mum, and in the process he teaches Will about the concept of family.

The First Wives Club, by Olivia Goldsmith (1991)

This entertaining novel was the basis for the popular movie, and for a fun beach read it can't be beat. Follow the high jinks of three jilted wives who decide to band together to punish the husbands who left them for younger models.

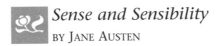

Sense and Sensibility

BY JANE AUSTEN

In this classic novel, the end of a love affair is chronicled in a way that seems as current as if it were written yesterday. In this scene, Marianne has just received a cold and formal letter from Willoughby, a man whom she thought was in love with her. Alas, it turns out he has found a wealthy woman to court and disavowed all his former feelings for Marianne, and all her letters to him have been returned. Here, she discusses her broken heart with her sister, Elinor.

"I felt myself," she added, "to be as solemnly engaged to him, as if the strictest legal covenant had bound us to each other."

"I can believe it," said Elinor; "but unfortunately he did not feel the same."

"He *did* feel the same, Elinor—for weeks and weeks he felt it. I know he did. Whatever may have changed him now (and nothing but the blackest art employed against me can have done it), I was once as dear to him as my own soul could wish. This lock of hair, which now he can so readily give up, was begged of me with the most earnest supplication. Had you seen his look, his manner, had you heard his voice at that moment! Have you forgot the last evening of our being together at Barton? The morning that we parted too! When he told me that it might be many weeks before we met again—his distress—can I ever forget his distress?"

For a moment or two she could say no more; but when this emotion had passed away, she added, in a firmer tone,

"Elinor, I have been cruelly used; but not by Willoughby."

"Dearest Marianne, who but himself? By whom can he have been instigated?"

"By all the world, rather than by his own heart. I could rather believe every creature of my acquaintance leagued together to ruin me in his opinion, than believe his nature capable of such cruelty. This woman of whom he writes—whoever she be—or any one, in short, but your own dear self, mama, and Edward, may have been so barbarous to bely me. Beyond you three, is there a creature in the world whom I would not rather suspect of evil than Willoughby, whose heart I know so well?"

Elinor would not contend, and only replied, "Whoever may have been so detestably your enemy, let them be cheated of their malignant triumph, my dear sister, by seeing how nobly the consciousness of your own innocence and good intentions supports your spirits. It is a reasonable and laudable pride which resists such malevolence."

"No, no," cried Marianne, "misery such as mine has no pride. I care not who knows that I am wretched. The triumph of seeing me so may be open to all the world. Elinor, Elinor, they who suffer little may be proud and independent as they like—may resist insult, or return mortification—but I cannot. I must feel—I must be wretched—and they are welcome to enjoy the consciousness of it that can."

"But for my mother's sake and mine—"

"I would do more than for my own. But to appear happy when I am so miserable—Oh! who can require it?"

Again they were both silent. Elinor was employed in walking thoughtfully from the fire to the window, from the window to the fire, without knowing that she received warmth from one, or discerning objects through the other; and Marianne, seated at the foot of the bed, with her head leaning against one of its posts, again took up Willoughby's letter, and, after shuddering over every sentence, exclaimed—

"It is too much! Oh, Willoughby, Willoughby, could this be yours! Cruel, cruel—nothing can acquit you. Elinor, nothing can. Whatever he might have heard against me—ought he not to have suspended his belief? Ought he not to have told me of it, to have given me the power of clearing myself? 'The lock of hair (repeating it from the letter), which you so obligingly bestowed on me'—That is unpardonable.

Willoughby, where was your heart when you wrote those words? Oh, barbarously insolent!— Elinor, can he be justified?"

"No, Marianne, in no possible way." ✖

CHAPTER VI

Learning About Love

All you need is love.
—John Lennon

All the miscellaneous quotes and stories that fall into a more general category than the previous chapters encompass are collected in this chapter, a veritable grab-bag of interesting facts and figures about love through the ages.

Learn some disturbing facts about love in the animal kingdom. Read about the derivation of such customs as Valentine's Day, the invention of the "heart shape" to signify romance, and many more fascinating tidbits about love and lovers, like why chocolate is "the food of love," why we call tomatoes "love apples," and even why the term "love" is used in tennis scoring.

Ever wonder what different flowers symbolize? You'll find an exhaustive list to help you decode just what that bouquet of flowers really means. There's also a section on great love scenes in movies, as well as an extensive list of video rental suggestions for all kinds of moods related to love.

Read stories of some of the crazy things people have done in the name of love. Learn to say "I love you" around the globe (always handy when you're traveling!). And add to your vocabulary some obscure (but real) words to dazzle your friends and family. Flip through this chapter for a good dose of general love knowledge.

> *Love makes the world go 'round.*
>
> —*Anonymous*

Love doesn't make the world go 'round. Love is what makes the ride worthwhile.

—Franklin P. Jones

A HISTORY OF VALENTINE'S DAY

The story of Valentine's Day is cloaked in mystery. Many people know that this holiday in February is said to commemorate the Catholic martyr St. Valentine, but even that simple statement leads to more questions than answers. In fact, the Catholic Church recognizes three different saints with the name Valentine or Valentinus.

One popular legend is that St. Valentine was a Roman priest in the third century A.D. who continued to perform marriages for young lovers, despite the royal decree of Emperor Claudius banning marriage. Legend has it that when Valentine's actions were discovered, the Emperor had him put to death. It may be his name that gives this lovers' holiday its patron saint, but we will never know for sure.

Still, whatever the initial reason for it, the 14th of February has long been celebrated as a day for lovers to proclaim their devotion to each other. Pope Gelasius declared February 14 to be known as "St. Valentine's Day" around A.D. 500. At that time, the prevailing "lottery" system for romantic pairing was deemed un-Christian and outlawed. The idea that couples could be joined on the basis of mutual affection was shocking and new, and by sanctioning a holiday specifically for wooing, the Church gave its stamp of approval to the concept of romantic love.

The oldest known Valentine still in existence today was written in 1415, and was penned by Charles, Duke of Orleans. He sent it to his wife while he was imprisoned in the Tower of London following his capture at the Battle of Agincourt. His Valentine poem can still be seen today in the manuscript collection of the British Library in London, England.

Valentine's Day began to be popularly celebrated in England around the seventeenth century. By the middle of the eighteenth century, it was common for friends and lovers both rich and poor to exchange small tokens of affection or handwritten notes expressing romantic feelings. By the end of the century, formal printed cards began to replace hand-written letters, since they were an easy way for people to express deep emotion without revealing too much personal feeling. Affordable postage also led to the popularity of sending Valentine's Day greetings. It took a bit longer for the valentine habit to spread across the ocean to the colonies, but by the mid-1700s, Americans were most likely exchanging handmade valentines like their counterparts in England.

In the 1840s, the first mass-produced valentines in America came from a sales effort led by one influential woman named Esther Howland (often called the "Mother of the American Valentine"). According to the Greeting Card Association, an estimated one billion valentine cards are sent each year, making Valentine's Day the second largest card-sending holiday of the year. (An estimated 2.6 billion cards are sent for Christmas.) Approximately 85 percent of all valentines are purchased by women. In addition to the United States and the United Kingdom, Valentine's Day is celebrated in Mexico, Australia, France, and Canada.

*Oh, my love is like a red, red
rose
That's newly sprung in June.
Oh my love is like the melody
That's sweetly play'd in tune.*

—Robert Burns

Victorian Valentines

These were found on antique postcards, but the sentiments here are as true today as they ever were. Steal one of these adorable poems for your own homemade valentine.

May this bow of white, which gives delight,
and which I send you, a token be of Love
divine, oh, wilt thou be My Valentine.

To My Valentine: Though Cupid's aim is true,
and piercing is his dart, I shall not mind, if
you, will give to me, your heart.

I could weather any storm
With your loving heart so warm.

I send to you this bow of golden hue
To tell you that my love is true
Be my Valentine, do!

Danny "Cutie" I am named,
For my deeds I'm widely famed
Every night and every day
Trusting hearts become my prey
Happy Valentine's Day!

Why beat around the bush at all,
Or be afraid to show it
When on someone love wants to call
Why not let someone know it.

Love conquers all; let us too yield to love.

—*Virgil*

SADIE HAWKINS' DAY

Sadie Hawkins' Day, which was especially popular in the late 1930s and '40s, was actually the invention of comic-strip artist Al Capp. His popular *L'il Abner* comic strip featured a character named Sadie Hawkins, described as "the homeliest gal in the hills." In mid-November of 1937, the strip featured a story about her father, a rich businessman in the town of Dogpatch, who decided to proclaim November 15 the First Annual "Sadie Hawkins' Day"—a foot race in which the spinsters of Dogpatch would run through the streets pursuing any unmarried men, with marriage as the prize to any girl lucky enough to bag a bachelor.

The idea for the event grabbed the public imagination, and by the late 1930s, a craze for

Sadie Hawkins events had swept the nation. *Life* magazine reported over 200 colleges holding such events in 1939, and at high schools and colleges across the nation, girls and women enjoyed the rare treat of being able to choose their own dates and do the asking for a change. In some ways, it was the earliest stirrings of the modern feminist movement.

Al Capp never intended his little comic strip plot to have such far-reaching consequences, but he dutifully kept it as a regular November event in his fictional town of Dogpatch for the remaining four decades he drew the strip.

*If you love something,
set it free; if it comes back
it's yours, if it doesn't,
it never was.*

—*Richard Bach*

*In her first passion,
woman loves her lover;
In all the others, all she
loves is love.*

—Lord Byron

Love, Said With Flowers

There are myriad meanings and definitions for different kinds of flowers, and many of these definitions have to do with love. Below, some special meanings for common flowers. If you create a bouquet using several of these, it's almost like writing a love letter without having to resort to something as mundane as mere words.

Anemone	Unfading love
Azalea	Fragile passion (also the Chinese symbol of womanhood)
Carnation (pink)	I'll never forget you
Carnation (red)	My heart aches for you; admiration
Chrysanthemum (yellow)	Slighted love

Coriander	Lust
Daisy	Innocence
Fern	Secret bond of love
Forget-me-not	True love; memories
Gardenia	You're lovely; secret love
Gladiolus	Love at first sight
Hyacinth (purple)	I'm sorry; please forgive me; sorrow
Jonquil	Your affection is returned
Lavender	Devotion
Mistletoe	Kiss me (also a sacred plant in India)
Moss	Maternal love; charity
Myrtle	Love (also the Hebrew emblem of marriage)
Orchid (cattleya)	Mature charm
Peony	Aphrodisiac
Primrose	I can't live without you

ROSES:

Rose (red)	Love ; I love you
Rose (white)	Eternal love; innocence

Rose (pink)	Perfect happiness; Please believe me
Rose (yellow)	Friendship
Rose (red and white)	Together; unity
Rose (thornless)	Love at first sight
Rose (single, full bloom)	I love you; I still love you
Spiderflower	Elope with me
Tulip (red)	Believe me; declaration of love
Tulip (variegated)	Beautiful eyes
Tulip (yellow)	Hopeless love
Violet (blue)	Watchfulness; faithfulness; I'll always be true
Violet (white)	Let's take a chance on happiness
Viscaria	Will you dance with me?
Zinnia (white)	Goodness

*Yet each man kills the
thing he loves,
By each let this be heard,
Some do it with a bitter look,
Some with a flattering word,
The coward does it with a kiss,
The brave man with a sword!*

—Oscar Wilde

"I LOVE YOU"
AROUND THE GLOBE

English	I love you.
Spanish	Te amo.
French	Je t'aime.
German	Ich liebe dich.
Japanese	Ai shite imasu.
Italian	Ti amo.
Chinese	Wo ai ni.
Swedish	Jag alskar.
Portuguese	Eu te amo.

For one human being to love another: that is perhaps the most difficult of our tasks; the ultimate, the last test and proof, the work for which all other work is but preparation.

—Rainer Maria Rilke

LOVE QUESTIONS AND ANSWERS

Q: Where does the use of the word "love" come from in tennis?

A: The word "love" to mean "no score" (in tennis, etc.) is dated from 1742, from the notion of "playing for love," i.e. "for nothing."

Q: Why do we use an "X" symbol to signify a kiss?

A: In medieval times, when many people could not read, they got into the habit of signing legal documents with a cross (X) to represent their signatures. In addition to signing a document, it was customary to kiss the signed document, just as one would kiss the Bible when taking an oath.

That's right, the phrase "sealed with a kiss" used to actually mean just what it sounds like—an oath or signature was considered legally binding once it had been kissed. Of course, since many people often didn't sign their names—instead using the aforementioned X symbol—someone signing a document would kiss the X in lieu of a signature. Over time the written X and the kiss became synonymous with each other.

Q: What was the first on-screen kiss in movies?

A: Amazingly enough, the very first film ever made featured a kiss. It was 1896, and Thomas Edison, working in his laboratory in Menlo Park, NJ, made a test movie to check out his new invention, the movie camera. In this short film—it was only one scene, really —viewers are treated to a coy Mrs. Edison sitting beside her husband as the two of them share a smooch.

Q: Why do we have the custom of kissing under the mistletoe?

A: Mistletoe is an old Celtic symbol of regeneration and eternal life, probably because mistletoe plants attach themselves to other living plants in order to live. The Romans valued it as a symbol of peace, which eventually led to its use as one of the symbolic decorations of Christmas. Kissing under mistletoe was a Roman custom, due to the plant being commonly regarded as a symbol of fertility.

Q: Why is Valentine's Day celebrated on February 14?

A: Some say that this date was once a pagan holiday that was co-opted by the church as a holiday with religious meaning. However, a more common theory holds that for some reason, February 14 was traditionally believed to be the day that birds chose their mates. Therefore, the day that doves and owls mated was a fine choice for a day that human beings would declare their own loving intentions.

Q: Why are tomatoes called "love apples"?

A: In Italy, the tomato was considered an aphrodisiac, perhaps because of its heart shape and juicy flesh. Because of this, the Italian word for tomato is poma amoris, which, literally translated, means "love apple."

Q: What is the longest marriage on record?

A: It's a tie! The longest marriages on record lasted 86 years, and in fact, there were two couples who can claim this record:

> Sir Timulji Nariman and Lady Nariman wed in 1853; each was five years old at the time.

Lazarus Rowe and Molly Webber married in 1743, both at the age of eighteen.

Q: Why is chocolate associated with love?

A: Throughout history, cocoa beans and chocolate have been valued, from the Aztecs to the modern day. Medical studies show that chocolate contains high levels of phenylethylamine, a natural chemical whose production by the brain can be triggered by such things as looking into the eyes of a significant other. An overdose of this "love molecule" causes a quickened heartbeat and sweaty palms—those physical, euphoric symptoms of falling in love. Perhaps this explains why chocolate is the leading Valentine's Day gift!

Generally, by the time you are Real, most of your hair has been loved off, and your eyes drop out and you get loose in the joints and very shabby. But these things don't matter at all, because once you are Real you can't be ugly, except to people who don't understand.

—*Margery Williams,*
The Velveteen Rabbit

THE HEART SHAPE

The familiar shape of a heart has become a sort of visual shorthand for love and romance, but how did this come to be? From ancient times, the heart was thought to be the source from which all human emotion springs, and so it is not surprising that artists tried to draw a shape they felt approximated the organ. Of course we now know that the heart is a muscle whose primary function is to pump blood through the body, but many vestigial traces remain in the language alluding to the heart as source of emotion. (You broke my heart; my heart is bleeding; my heart aches for you; etc.)

It is not known when the valentine heart shape became the familiar symbol for "heart"— and thanks to modern science and medicine, we know that an actual heart is much more like the shape of a closed fist. Perhaps early artists guessed at the shape of the heart, and the common mirror image of two curves that we know today as "heart-shaped" was just a lucky stroke of design whimsy.

> *Love: Two minds without a single thought.*
>
> —*Philip Barry*

*Love is being
stupid together.*

—*Paul Valery*

Ten Famous Love Scenes of the Silver Screen

At its best, there's something about the experience of sitting in a darkened theater, watching the actors on a stage or screen, which cannot be duplicated by anything in the "real world." Surrounded by other people, we still manage to forge a very personal one-on-one relationship with the characters that mirror our own lives. Of course, any list of great love scenes is naturally going to leave a lot out, because this is only a small sampling of all the wonderful moments that Hollywood has given us. Think about your own ten favorites.

The Thin Man (1934)

Throughout almost 15 years of "Thin Man" movies, Nick (William Powell) and Nora (Myrna Loy) Charles were consistently one of the most engaging and electric couples to hit the screen. In the first of their films, based on the Dashiell Hammett novel, there is a lovely moment that is representative of all the wise-cracking and affection seen throughout. Nick and Nora are throwing a party, and Nick has retired to his office with an attractive young woman who wants him to investigate the disappearance of her father. Filled with fear and strong emotion, she throws herself into his arms, at the very same moment his wife appears at the door of the room. For a moment, it looks as if a big misunderstanding is about to take place, the sort of scene we've seen a thou-

sand times, where the jealous wife miscon-
strues an innocent moment. But no, instead
Nick Charles makes a goofy face at his wife,
who responds in kind, and in that single beat,
the audience sees a demonstration of the
absolute trust and humor that is the founda-
tion of their marriage.

Gone With the Wind (1939)

Gone with the Wind is perhaps the definitive
archetype of a certain kind of larger-than-life
love story. Scores of movies followed in its foot-
steps to portray the dashing unavailable man
and the fiery independent woman who can't
admit that she loves him, but this epic film, a
four-hour adaptation of the Margaret Mitchell
novel, did it first and best. When Rhett Butler
(Clark Gable) finally confesses his love to

Scarlett O'Hara (Vivian Leigh) as the fires of Atlanta burn in the background, he tells her "I've loved you more than I've ever loved any woman. I've waited longer for you than I've ever waited for any woman," and their passionate kiss practically burns up the screen.

Casablanca (1942)

This film is perhaps the most enduring love story of all time. Consistently on critics' top-ten lists, it tells the story of nightclub owner Rick (Humphrey Bogart) and Ilsa (Ingrid Bergman), the woman from his past who appears in his bar one night. When she leaves at the end of the movie, he delivers some of the most memorable lines ever uttered by a lover sending his beloved away forever. "Ilsa, I'm no good at being noble, but it doesn't take much to see that the problems of three little people don't amount to a hill of beans in this crazy world. Someday you'll understand that. Now, now. . . Here's looking at you kid."

From Here to Eternity (1953)
Set against the backdrop of WWII, with the attack on Pearl Harbor still ahead, this movie examines the friendships and hopes of a group of military men stationed in Hawaii. Especially notable is the torrid—yet forbidden—love affair between First Sergeant Milton Warden (Burt Lancaster) and the wife (Deborah Kerr) of his commanding officer. Their flirtation culminates in one of the steamiest love scenes of the '50s, where they embrace on the beach, knowing that if they are ever caught, all hell will break loose.

The Graduate (1967)

Benjamin (Dustin Hoffman) is a young man just out of college, trying to figure out what to do next. But what he didn't plan for is an affair with a seductive older woman. Mrs. Robinson (Anne Bancroft) taps into every young man's fantasy of being taught "the ropes" of love and sex by an experienced teacher. And when he first realizes her less-than-aboveboard intentions, who can forget his innocent yet excited query: "Mrs. Robinson, are you trying to seduce me?"

Love Story (1970)

This film was based on the popular novel by Erich Segal, and follows the romance between rich preppie Oliver (Ryan O'Neal) and music major Jenny (Ali MacGraw). Oliver's father disapproves of his match, and the young couple must start a life with small material wealth but great richness of love for one another. Unfortunately, when she tries to conceive a child she receives a shocking diagnosis, and this three-hanky movie could cause a stone to cry, especially when Oliver plaintively says one of the most oft-quoted lines in popular culture: "Love means never having to say you're sorry."

When Harry Met Sally . . . (1989)
Who can forget Sally (Meg Ryan) shocking Harry (Billy Crystal)—not to mention all the patrons of the diner where they are having lunch—when she demonstrates to him just how easy it is for a woman to fake an orgasm? But of course the true love scene in the movie occurs at the end, as Harry races through the

festive city streets on New Year's Eve to find Sally and profess his love.

Beautiful Thing (1996)

This English movie chronicles the awakening love between two boys in an East London housing project. The film's final scene celebrates the triumphant "coming out" of Jamie and Ste, as they dance exuberantly together to the strains of Mama Cass in front of all their neighbors. . . . It's a sweet, triumphant scene that warms the hearts of anyone, straight or gay, who has every experienced the flush of first love.

Jerry Maguire (1996)

This romantic comedy showed a brash young businessman learning to let himself fall in love—and mean it. Theaters full of women swooned when Jerry (Tom Cruise) appeared at the door and proclaimed to Dorothy (Renée Zellweger), "I love you. You . . . complete me," and she uttered the famous line, "Shut up. Just shut up. You had me at hello."

Titanic (1997)

This fictional love story set on the historically ill-fated *Titanic* ship features the romantic but doomed affair between the impoverished Jack Dawson (Leonardo DiCaprio) and the rich-but-unhappy heiress, Rose DeWitt Bukater (Kate Winslet). When Jack saves her from an impulsive suicide bid, he tells her, "I'm not looking forward to jumping in after you. But like I said, I don't see a choice. I guess I'm kinda hoping you'll come back over the rail and get me off the hook here," and before you know it, he's wrapping her in his arms as audiences swoon.

MORE GREAT LOVE SCENES

Tarzan the Ape Man (1932)
> Love story, jungle-style, and contains the unforgettable line "Me Tarzan, You Jane." Love doesn't get any more basic than that!

A Star is Born (1937, 1954, 1976)
> Pick any one of 'em, they're all romantic as hell.

Notorious (1946)
> It has the best kissing scene in a film, the one with Cary Grant and Ingrid Bergman on the balcony.

Brief Encounter (1946)

A doomed love affair in black and white, very English, very proper, very romantic.

Roman Holiday (1953)

Audrey Hepburn is luminous, and the backdrop of Rome, is romantic as it gets!

Desk Set (1957)

Classic love story with Hepburn and Tracy— and who doesn't love a sexy librarian?

An Affair to Remember (1957)

This romantic favorite was the basis for *Sleepless in Seattle*, another beloved romance, but why not rent the original?

Truffaut's *Jules and Jim* (1962), Godard's *Breathless* (1960), and Godard's *My Life to Live* (1962)

A trio of New Wave films with many classic moments of doomed romance.

Harold and Maude (1971)

A non-traditional love story, for sure, but sweetly romantic and a good reminder that sometimes love comes in unexpected packages.

Grease (1978)

The story of Danny and Sandy's love for each other is timeless, in a kitschy 1970s version of the 1950s kind of way.

Out of Africa (1985)

One of those to-die-for romances, with Meryl Streep, and Robert Redford in possibly his most hunky role ever.

A Room With a View (1986)

The utterly legendary Merchant/Ivory film, with everybody's favorite screen hunk, Julian Sands.

The English Patient (1996)

Romance, war, deserts, caves, and passion—lots of passion.

The Princess Bride (1987)

A classic fairy tale, which wouldn't be complete without the obligatory, excellently romantic love story between a fair maiden and a handsome hero.

Do the Right Thing (1989)

That excellent love scene with Spike Lee and Rosie Perez.

Pretty Woman (1990)

A Cinderella story set in the modern business world.

Flirting (1991)

This under-appreciated Australian gem features a young Nicole Kidman, and has some of the best scenes of young love, repression, and longing.

Impromptu (1991)

An all-star cast playing famous writers and musicians of the nineteenth century, this movie is not only a romantic powerhouse but also features some of the best classical music as a soundtrack.

Desperado (1995)

Best movie sex: Antonio Banderas and Salma Hayek—hot!

Boys Don't Cry (1999)

Some excellent romantic moments amidst a horrifyingly depressing true story.

Don't forget Woody Allen! Both *Annie Hall* (1977) and *Manhattan* (1979) are quite romantic!

However dull a woman may be, she will understand all there is in love; however intelligent a man may be, he will never know but half of it.

—Madame Feé

Man cannot degrade woman without himself falling into degradation; he cannot elevate her without at the same time elevating himself.

—Alexander Walker

LABORS OF LOVE

What's the most ridiculous thing you ever did in the name of love?

"Moved across the country . . . and then it didn't work out with her and I was stranded."

"Carried the tent, the food, and all our stuff so that my boyfriend could carry his sound equipment when we traveled to Australia, so he could record the sound of the ocean in western Australia. Picture him walking along with a microphone and a shoulder bag with a tape recorder, and me with a backpack almost as heavy as I was, scuttling along behind him being, careful not to fall over backward from the huge weight I was carrying."

"Well, I didn't actually do it, but I came very close to rear-ending someone with my car just to have an excuse to talk to him. It was someone I had a crush on, and I happened to be stopped behind him at a traffic light, and I seriously pondered just giving his car a little tap. I didn't do it, though."

"I dropped out of college for a girl, then told her sister I was actually in love with her (the sister, that is). Didn't end up with either of them—and I was broke and a college dropout to boot!"

"I signed up for a small senior-level philosophy seminar in college because I heard that the guy I had a crush on was taking it. When I showed up for the first class, it appeared he had dropped the class, so I went right to the registrar and dropped it as well."

> *Love is a perky elf dancing a merry little jig and then suddenly he turns on you with a miniature machine gun.*
>
> —Matt Groening

CREEPY CRAWLY LOVE

In the insect and animal kingdom, mating rituals can seem quite odd—if not downright painful—when looked at through the lens of human culture.

Female Bola spiders attract their prey by playing at romance: The spider sends out a pheromone that mimics the sex attraction hormone of the moth. Male moths respond to this pheromone scent in the air, and come flying to find its source, only to be hit with a sticky ball of silk that the spider has carefully created. The spider hits him with the ball of silk, which paralyzes the poor moth, and then feeds on her captive. He was only looking for a little love!

The female blue crab sends out her pheromone to attract a mate, and if the male is attracted enough, he performs a little dance by rising up on his rear walking legs and shaking his front claws. Once the female sees this and is attracted enough to come over to him, he grabs her and attaches her to the bottom of his shell and carries her around like that for a few days, almost like a barnacle on the bottom of a ship. A few days later, she molts; at that point, they copulate. Generally, this is the only mating experience in the life of a female blue crab.

For the male praying mantis, sexual contact is fraught with danger. After mating, the female praying mantis sometimes eats her mate, starting with the head. The male praying mantis continues mating even though his head is gone! He may know that this is the last chance for sex he will ever have.

The common bedbug has one of the most painful-seeming mating rituals: The male bedbug actually pierces the female in order to create a cavity in which to deposit sperm.

> *Love teaches even asses to dance.*
>
> —*French Proverb*

Neither a lofty degree of intelligence nor imagination nor both together go to the making of genius. Love, love, love, that is the soul of genius.

—Mozart

Obscure Words of Love

This is just a small sampling of English words relating to love and sex that are rarely used, but really ought to be dusted off and put to work again.

Agrexophrenia: Sexual dysfunction caused by a fear that you will be overheard having sex.

Amychesis: Scratching one's partner's back during the sexual act without realizing it.

Callipygian: Having pleasantly shaped buttocks.

Gamomania: A form of insanity that is manifested by the making of ridiculous marriage proposals.

Gerontophelia: A sexual fetish for elderly males.

Imparlibidinous: The case of partners having an unequal sexual desire.

Lovertine: One who is addicted to sex.

Nanophilia: A sexual fetish for short people.

Nympholepsy: A trance caused by an erotic daydream.

Paphian: Pertaining to an illicit love, lewd.

Pinchpin: A married woman who continually demands that her husband satisfy her sexually.

Pornocracy: A government by prostitutes.

Smellsmock: A lecherous man.

Tarassis: A hysterical condition of males.

Uxurious: Overly fond of one's wife.

Viraginity: A descriptive term for a mannish woman (not to be confused with "virginity").

*To the world
you may be one person,
but to one person
you may be the world.*

—Anonymous

*Age does not protect
you from love
but love to some extent
protects you from age.*

—*Jeanne Moreau*

Bibliography

Aesop, *The Fables of Aesop*, Dover Books, Toronto, ©2002.

Barron's, *The Traveler's Phrase Book*, Barron's Educational Series, New York, ©2001.

Brasch, B., *How Did It Begin?*, Pocket Books, New York, ©1969 (orig. published in 1966 by The David McKay Co.).

Davidoff, Henry, ed., *The Pocket Book Of Quotations*, Pocket Books, New York, ©1942.

Engelmeier, Peter W. ed., *Happy Together: Hollywood's Unforgettable Couples*, Prestel Publishers, Munich, ©2002.

Fone, Byrne ed., *The Columbia Anthology of Gay Literature*, Columbia Press, New York, ©1998.

Hanley, Jack. *Let's Make Mary: Being A Gentleman's Guide To Scientific Seduction In 8 Easy Lessons*, Phoenix Press, New York, ©1937.

Hubbard, Elberd, *Elbert Hubbard's Scrapbook, Containing The Inspired And Inspiring Selections Gathered During A Lifetime*, Wm. Wise and Co, New York, ©1923.

Hunt, John, ed., *365 Love Poems*, Barnes & Noble Books, New York, ©1993.

Marvell, Andrew, *To His Coy Mistress and Other Poems*, Dover Books, Toronto, ©1997.

Novobatzky, Peter, and Ammon Shea, *Depraved English*, St. Martin's Press, New York, ©1999.

Robinson, Edward Arlington, *Miniver Cheevy and Other Poems,* Dover Books, New York, ©1995.

Shakespeare, William, *The Sonnets*, Signet Books, New York, ©1964.

Sonntag, Linda, *Seduction through the Ages*, Sterling Publishing, New York, ©2001.

Washington, Peter, ed., *Comic Poems*, Everyman Library, Alfred A. Knopf, ©2001.

Washington, Peter, ed., *Love Letters*, Everyman Library, Alfred A. Knopf, ©1996.

Index